M000035803

DESIGN FOR TEA

Tea Wares from the Dragon Court to Afternoon Tea

JANE PETTIGREW

SUTTON PUBLISHING

First published in 2003 by
Sutton Publishing Limited · Phoenix Mill
Thrupp · Stroud · Gloucestershire · GL5 2BU

Copyright © Jane Pettigrew, 2003

All rights reserved. No part of this publication may be reproduced, stored in a
retrieval system, or transmitted, in any form, or by any means, electronic,
mechanical, photocopying, recording or otherwise, without prior permission
of the publisher and copyright holder.

Jane Pettigrew has asserted the moral right to be identified as the author of
this work.

British Library Cataloguing in Publication Data
A catalogue record for this book is available from the British Library

ISBN 0 7509 3283 X

Typeset in 12/17 pt Caslon.
Typesetting and origination by
Sutton Publishing Limited.
Printed and bound in England by
J.H. Haynes & Co. Ltd, Sparkford.

Contents

Acknowledgements

I would like to express my sincere thanks to the following who loaned pictures to illustrate the text:

Stephen Twining for material from the Twining archives; Leo Kwan for his beautiful pictures of Yixing teapots and his help with contacts in China and Hong Kong; Andrew Demmer for images from his collection of historic caddies, Austria; John Pearman for images of teapots and teacups and illustrations from his treasured J.C. Vickery's catalogue; Jeremy and Stephen Stodel for images of British, American and Chinese silver tea wares; Joan Jones at Royal Doulton Museum & Archives, UK; Jacqueline Banks of The Royal Crown Derby Museum, UK; Lynn Miller at The Wedgwood Museum, UK; Everson Hall of the Hall China Company, USA; The Tea Council, London.

Thanks also go to:

Gilles Brochard, President of Le Club des Buveurs de Thé in Paris for helping me to find contacts in France; Honey Tilly, for the loan of her silver tea wares for photography; Chris Lacey at The National Trust Photographic Library;

Martin Durrant at The Victoria & Albert Images Picture Agency; John Beckerson and Christopher Garibaldi at Norwich Castle Museum; and Elaine English at the Museum of Domestic Architecture.

I would also like to thank the following for permission to reproduce extracts from their publications:

The National Trust for extracts from Lesley Lewis, *The Private Life of a Country House, 1912–1939*, 1980
Doubleday, New York, for extracts from *Vogue's Book of Etiquette*
Tea & Coffee Trade Journal, New York, USA for extracts from William Ukers, *All About Tea*

And, finally, thanks also for the following:

Extracts from *Lark Rise to Candleford* by Flora Thompson (1945) reprinted by permission of Oxford University Press
Extracts from *Moveable Feasts* by Arnold Palmer (1952) reprinted by permission of Oxford University Press
Extracts from *Life in a Noble Household* by Gladys Scott Thomson published by Hutchinson. Used by permission of The Random House Group Limited. *British Tastes: An Enquiry into the Likes and Dislikes of the Regional Consumer* by David Elliston published by Hutchinson. Used by permission of The Random House Group Limited.

Every effort has been made to contact other copyright holders. The author will be glad to make good in future any errors or omissions brought to her attention.

Introduction

Each time we measure tea leaves into a teapot or lift a cup to sip the refreshing brew we become another link in the fascinating chain of events that connects the modern tea-drinking world to ancient China. Every part of our daily lives and the way in which we do certain things, perform certain rituals, are connected in some way to what has gone before. In our eating and drinking habits, we behave in certain ways and use certain table wares without necessarily knowing why, and it is only by exploring the past that the connections become clearer. Why, for example, are teapots round and squat and not tall and narrow like coffee pots? Why is a teacup shallow and bowl-shaped when the coffee cup has always maintained its straight sides and deeper form? Why is the box in which we store our tea called a caddy? And why is British-style afternoon tea served at low side-tables in the drawing room rather than round the dining table in the kitchen or dining room?

The answers to all these questions may be found in the 5,000-year history of tea-drinking that began in China in 2737 BC, travelled to Japan in the ninth century and reached Europe in the 1600s. It is the development and use of tea-time furniture, porcelains, silverwares and linens that directly resulted from tea's fascinating journey from East to West that I have tried to discover in this book.

The story starts in China, where the tea plant was first cultivated and manufactured to give a brew that was found to be refreshing, sustaining and beneficial to the national health. The mythical figure Emperor Shen Nung, who is said to have discovered tea's medicinal powers, encouraged the creation of new plantations in his land and urged his people to drink tea because it 'gives vigour to the body, contentment to the mind and determination to the purpose'. Another ancient Chinese philosopher recommended 'Drink tea that your mind may be lively and clear'.

With the growing passion among the Chinese for green tea came generous pottery bowls from which to drink it, but these were gradually refined and developed into exquisite translucent little bowls when the Chinese potters started making porcelain. These fine drinking vessels migrated to Europe along with teapots, tea jars and tea. The correct brewing of tea in the time of the Tang Dynasty (AD 618–906) involved twenty-seven pieces of special equipment, but the pots, jars and bowls were the only three to be adopted by those in the West. However, even the utensils that were less relevant to Europeans and therefore not imported by them are still connected in some way to Western tea wares. The brazier to boil the water in China became in Europe the silver kettle with its own little burner. The Mongolian firepot that sits on top of a charcoal burner travelled to Russia and was called a samovar. The Chinese tea scoop was perhaps equivalent to the caddy spoon. The basket that held a complete set of Chinese tea-brewing and drinking equipment developed in the West as the tea tray. And the bamboo carryall used by the Chinese to store and transport tea wares perhaps became the tea hamper that allows afternoon tea to travel to any chosen location. Those three important pieces of equipage that were adopted – the teapot, the porcelain tea canister and the tea bowl – gradually, over the centuries, became so much a part of European customs that many people would never realise the connection with China. Both the chummy round teapots used at breakfast and the more elegant pots that grace the afternoon tea table are almost identical in form and use to the earliest Chinese earthenware brewing pots. And the teacups and saucers used in Europe and North America today are direct descendants from the Chinese originals. Yes, they acquired a handle, but the shape has changed very little. And the caddy in use today originated as a tall porcelain jar from China and took a Malay word as its name. Like all travellers, these vital pieces of the tea equipment have been adapted, developed, changed as they have come into contact with other cultures, but the basics have remained the same.

Some tea-time table wares were born independently of the Chinese and Japanese traditions, growing instead from patterns of food consumption or meal-time etiquette in the different countries where tea became popular. For example, neither the mote spoon nor the tea cosy (both important at the tea table at one time or another in both England and North America) has any link at all with China or Japan. The mote skimmer was an inventive adaptation of an ordinary teaspoon to allow the removal of unsightly tea leaves from the cup. Perhaps at first it was a practical utensil with its holes punched in the bowl, devised to meet the fastidious table manners of the English withdrawing room of the eighteenth century. Then, with the refined art of the silversmiths, it grew from being merely a useful tool to become one of the most appealingly elegant and charming pieces of the tea equipage. The Chinese would not understand this desire to skim floating tea leaves out of the cup, since they often brew their tea in the glass or cup from which it is drunk. Similarly, the cosy was a quirky piece of Victorian common sense crossbred with an indulgent approach to decorative objects and home furnishings and nothing at all to do with tea-drinking in China. Although often designed in Britain with Japanese or Chinese style in mind, cosies are not an Oriental part of the tea ceremony.

The way in which different pieces of tea ware are used and the location in which tea is served have also developed for different reasons – sometimes because an idea or piece of table ware has been imported and its use perpetuated, sometimes because a new idea has developed to suit our own environment. The brewing of loose-leaf tea in a round-bodied vessel with a handle and spout, for instance, is performed in Europe and North America in exactly the same way as in China at the time of the Qing Dynasty

(1644–1800). Travellers and merchants who had visited China and Japan and had come across the unknown herb and the customs and rituals associated with it talked about and wrote about what they had seen and experienced. Others inevitably wished to try the same experience for themselves, if not from simple curiosity then just to make sure they kept up with latest trends and knew as much about new fashions as their friends and neighbours did. And if they could not actually visit China or Japan, they at least wanted to try the new beverage using the correct vessel and the same little bowls.

On the other hand, lockable tea chests came into being not because the Chinese used such chests but because of the high cost of tea in Europe and the need to protect it from greedy servants. However, those secure chests were designed to keep safe the tea jars that had gradually evolved from tall, straight-sided Oriental porcelain tea jars. And the endless discussion in Britain, and elsewhere, as to whether the milk should be poured into the tea or the tea into the milk is not a conversation that would have taken place in China or Japan since in neither country is milk added to the green tea drunk there. In England, the early use of milk led to a daily habit that has hardly changed in 300 years.

So the adoption, adaptation, evolution and invention of all the items required in the preparation and service of tea weave a fascinating and meandering trail through all the tea-drinking countries, throwing up questions and mysteries that challenge and intrigue.

If the universal story of tea wares started in ancient China, my own enchantment with beautiful tea wares started at my grandmother's house, where afternoon tea was served every Saturday and Sunday with all the proper ceremony, even when I was small and quite likely to drop or spill one of the precious porcelain cups. It was perfectly normal for the best white-and-gold tea service to be laid out ready with pearl-handled tea knives and embroidered napkins, as well as a fold-out wooden cake stand bearing sandwiches, hot buttered muffins (in winter, we toasted our own over the glowing coal fire), home-made cakes and biscuits. The thin, shiny porcelain was so gloriously elegant, so perfectly fashioned and so expensive-looking that, for me, tea time transformed us all into lords and ladies, princes and princesses. I still have the gold tea set and use it with great pride whenever anyone comes to tea. 'It was my Grandmother's,' I announce, knowing that the tea will taste far better because of its connections to Edwardian tea parties.

The next stage in my awareness of the importance of tea and tea wares came when two friends and I opened a tea shop called Tea-Time in Clapham in south-west London. In our Art Deco setting, we wanted to re-create the charm of the 1930s, when going out to tea was still an important part of many people's social life in Britain. And so we started hunting in antique markets and fairs for all the things we needed to serve tea 'properly' – embroidered and lace tablecloths, cake stands, cups and saucers, teapots, hot-water jugs, strainers, tea knives, teaspoons, sugar bowls and milk jugs. When the tables were all set up on a busy day, the room looked lovely, inviting, welcoming and nostalgically smile-provoking. The reaction from our customers, as they poured their tea through a tea strainer, helped themselves to scones from a pretty basket or hand-painted cake plate and spread their jam and cream using a neat little tea knife with a coloured handle that matched the china, was pleasing. They often remarked to us that they were determined to go home, climb up into their attic and find their own traditional tea things, which had been hidden away, so that they could once again serve tea in the old-fashioned way.

Since 1983, when we opened Tea-Time, there has been an almost universal revival of interest in tea and what it can offer us in the modern world. In Britain, hotels and tea shops compete each year to be the best in the country. In the USA, there are new tea shops and tea rooms opening up all over the country with conferences and training programmes attracting people from all walks of life. In Japan, British-style tea shops punctuate the rows of stores in malls in all the major cities, and scones and clotted cream are served in time-honoured English fashion. Instead of always drinking their traditional green tea, the Japanese now also drink black, with milk, to accompany their afternoon tea. In France, Italy, Spain, Scandinavia, Russia, Hungary and

Poland, new retail stores offer a wide range of loose tea, and five-star hotels serve afternoon tea. In a world where communication between different cultures is easier, faster and always revealing something new, there is a constant intermingling of ideas, and tea is there among the experiences that inspire.

Without having to discuss the pleasures involved, people seem to sense the 'zen' of the tea ceremony. They find, when they take the trouble to assemble the relevant utensils, focus on what they are doing and why they are doing it, that their sense of refreshment is not purely because of the drink. It comes also from the ritual, from the deep sense of satisfaction and appreciation of beautiful things used in harmony with each other to create a quiet time of spiritual renewal. And with a greater understanding of a history that stretches back thousands of years, that enjoyment of the tea things is as great as the satisfaction we derive from the beverage itself. I hope that this book will widen all tea-drinkers' perspective on their own tea rituals and bring greater pleasure to all their tea-drinking occasions.

1930s 'Balmoral' teapot made by Burleigh. (*Author's Collection*)

1

earthenware teapots from China

'Priests' Hats and Lotus Flowers'

The origins of tea and tea-drinking lie deep in China's history and so, in all the countries around the world where tea has played an important social role, Chinese design and craftsmanship guided the development of the vessels in which the herb was carefully and lovingly brewed.

Through the early centuries of Chinese tea-drinking, the leaves were variously boiled fresh in a pan of water; dried, powdered and boiled; steamed, powdered, made into little dry cakes and then boiled; powdered and whisked into hot water in a bowl; or dried and then steeped in hot or boiling water. There was no need for a teapot until the reign of the Ming Dynasty from 1368 to 1644, when this last method of infusing the processed leaves became fashionable. And with the change in brewing fashion came the change in equipment. The inventive Chinese took their ancient idea of a pot with spout and handle that was used for wine and water, and transformed it into an infuser for tea. And just as the wine ewer had been shaped to imitate animals, flowers and native plants, so the manufacture of desirable teapots continued in this beautifully creative tradition.

I

Chinensis cum olla cui incoquuntur folia The

The Chinensis cum herbe

TRACTATVS

DE

CHINENSIVM THE'

CAP. I.

De natura Thé, de nomine ejus, locis è quibus affertur & usus ejus antiquitate.

ERLUSTRATA natura Café, Chinensium *Thé* nunc aggredimur, inter ista enim non minima est convenientia. Ut Arabiæ Café ita Chinæ Thé debemus; ejusdem sunt amaritudinis; eodem penè tem-

E 3

An illustration from a book in Latin by Dufour on tea, coffee and chocolate, 1685.

As one anonymous seventeenth-century Chinese writer explained, 'Teapots were made in the form of many things, such as the water chestnut flower, the narcissus, the hollyhock, the chrysanthemum, a tortoise, a bird, a wheel, a drum, a goose's egg, an olive, a pumpkin, the nose of a foreign elephant, shark's skin, a Buddhist priest's hat, a lotus seed case, the drooping lotus flower, the joints of bamboo, a square flat goblet of the Han Dynasty, a wine jar with the handle overhead, and the beaker.' Looking back in 1890 over centuries of teapot manufacture, Richard Banister wrote in his *Cantor Lectures on Sugar, Coffee, Tea, and Cocoa: Their Origin, Preparation, and Uses*:

In the Far East the teapot has been an article of common household use nearly back to the sixth century. It is where the artist artisans are constantly inspired by the sight of the low, compact, glossy little shrub and its strangely fragrant white blossoms, and are cheered by the pale decoction of its leaves, that one must look for the fullest and finest expression of ideas in the form and decoration of teapots. . . . The constant and more common use of the teapot in the household led toward a lower and broader vase or body for the vessel, and the opening at the top, or cover, kept enlarging in diameter until there have been reached those Chinese teapots whose spouts and handles alone save them from being covered cups.

The most exquisite of those imaginative and inspired pots arrived in Europe from the town of Yixing (pronounced yeeshing), which lies to the west of Shanghai in Jiangsu Province in north-eastern China. The clay deposits in this unique location vary in colour from the famous 'purple sand' to rich deep black-browns, glistening greens, deep earthy reds and umbers to paler browns, golds and ochres. The potteries here have been making glazed and unglazed earthenwares since 2500 BC and the pots are still prized today for their ability

A Yixing pot made by Chinese artist Chen Guo-Liang. The style is 'Yuan-zhu'. The red earthenware is said vastly to improve the quality of the infusion. (*Leo Kwan*)

with the lavish oriental custom of gifts. For a dozen years past there have been sporadic cases of the teapot fever, until it is now a recognized form of collectors' mania. The average tourist, especially if the tourist is a woman, is now sure to

EVOLUTION OF THE TEAPOT.

bring home from Europe a few or a great many oddly shaped spoons as souvenirs. The round-the-world traveller, the " globe trotter," as she is termed in all the region between Suez and San Francisco, brings

OWARI.

one or more teapots if she brings anything from the far East. Teapot collectors are now nearly as numerous in the great circling army of globe trotters as are amateur photographers, the collector and the kodaker always exhibiting a little surprise and dismay to find that any of his particular kind have gone before him. Few of these tourist collections are worthy of

NABESHIMA WARE. JAPANESE.

much consideration, as time, knowledge and discrimination are most necessary to every pursuit and more particularly in the Orient. Where there have been better conditions a collection of teapots is quite as interesting, curious and valuable as any other treasury of industrial art.

Everyone who lives in the Orient makes his collection of something quaint, artistic, obsolete, useful or instructive. It is inevitable and climatic, and the strongest minds, holding out for years, finally yield

and suffer the mania in its severest form. In Japan the collector's craze is in the very air and soil, and there were collecting enthusiasts back to the days of Jingu Kogo. Every Japanese gentleman has his collection of some kind, either secret or acknowledged, and the scale

COMPARISON OF JAPANESE GOURD TEAPOT AND PERSIAN WATER POT.

ranges from the most superb accumulations of netsukes, inros, kakemonos, crystals, lacquer, armor, swords, porcelains, faience, bronzes, brocades, embroideries, costumes, pipes, temple accessories, coins and autographs, down to shells, ferns, flowers, plants, rabbits, goldfish, Tosa chickens, and the latter-day postage stamp.

OLD MING. CHINESE.

A collection of teapots might be made in Europe, but occidental potters and metal workers have not shown much ingenuity in adapting their ideas to the tea ceremony, and comparatively little originality in these three hundred years since

HANGKOW. CHINESE.

the Dutch first brought the leaf from the Orient. In the far East the teapot has been an article of common household use

CANTON PUZZLE POT.

nearly back to the sixth century. It is where the artist artisans are constantly inspired by the sight of the low, compact, glossy little shrub and its strangely

A page from an essay entitled 'Collections of Teapots' by Eliza Ruhamah Scidmore, published in Richard Banister's *Cantor Lectures on Sugar, Coffee, Tea, and Cocoa: Their Origin, Preparation, and Uses*, 1890.

Mr and Mrs Hill by Arthur Devis (1711–87), showing their little red earthenware teapot among the Chinese porcelains on the elegant tea table, *c.* 1750. (*Bridgeman Art Library*)

to allow the tea flavour to develop more fully and to keep the tea hot for longer than porcelain seems able to do. In 1685, having read an advertising paper on Chinese teapots, Peter Muguet wrote, 'The Chinese teapots are made from a reddish clod of earth or impressed clay, in which they think that the tea is best made perfect. Whether that is so I do not know. But certainly

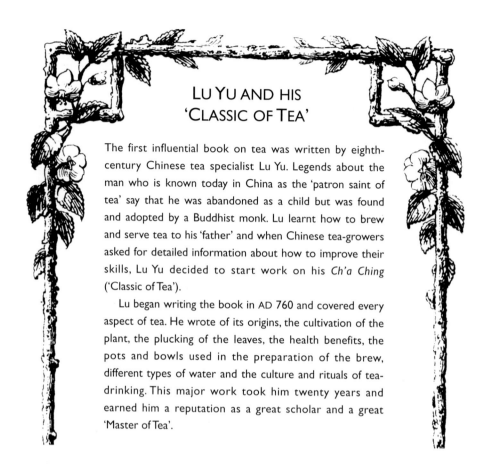

LU YU AND HIS 'CLASSIC OF TEA'

The first influential book on tea was written by eighth-century Chinese tea specialist Lu Yu. Legends about the man who is known today in China as the 'patron saint of tea' say that he was abandoned as a child but was found and adopted by a Buddhist monk. Lu learnt how to brew and serve tea to his 'father' and when Chinese tea-growers asked for detailed information about how to improve their skills, Lu Yu decided to start work on his *Ch'a Ching* ('Classic of Tea').

Lu began writing the book in AD 760 and covered every aspect of tea. He wrote of its origins, the cultivation of the plant, the plucking of the leaves, the health benefits, the pots and bowls used in the preparation of the brew, different types of water and the culture and rituals of tea-drinking. This major work took him twenty years and earned him a reputation as a great scholar and a great 'Master of Tea'.

the depiction of them at the beginning of this treatise shows that they are most elegant.'

As more and more people around England came across these wares, the Chinese teapots found their way into grand homes all over the country. In July 1693, for their home at Kingston Hall (now Kingston Lacy) in Devon, the Bankes family 'pay'd for a red China teapot 10/-, for 6 tea dishes & sugar box 12/-, for 4 coffee dishes 6/-', and in August of the same year, Mr Bankes 'pay'd for a brown earthenware teapot 2/6', as the household accounts reveal.

Once the European potteries started copying the form and style of the Yixing earthenwares, and as porcelain eventually became more available, the original redware Chinese pots were less evident on the tea table. But now, with the growing interest in tea and its Oriental links, these exquisite hand-made pots are reappearing in tea shops around the world. Yixing potters still make them using the traditional methods and the same skill. The pots have not changed in size or shape, the balance of the proportions is still important and the decoration can be extremely simple or more complex, involving creative and realistic effects of tree bark, bundled bamboo, lotus seeds, dragons or knotted cloth. The craftsmanship of today is so similar to that displayed several hundred years ago that most people would find it very difficult to distinguish a seventeenth-century pot from one made in the twenty-first century.

The pots are still unglazed and therefore rather porous and are generally used only for one particular type of tea. The absorption of the tea flavour

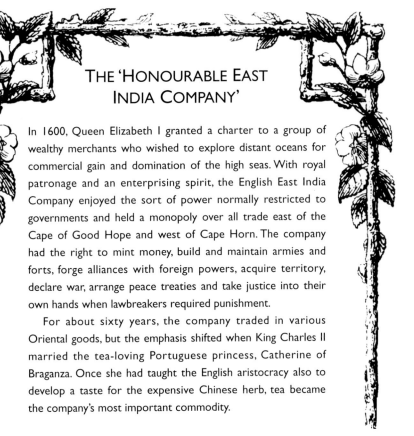

THE 'HONOURABLE EAST INDIA COMPANY'

In 1600, Queen Elizabeth I granted a charter to a group of wealthy merchants who wished to explore distant oceans for commercial gain and domination of the high seas. With royal patronage and an enterprising spirit, the English East India Company enjoyed the sort of power normally restricted to governments and held a monopoly over all trade east of the Cape of Good Hope and west of Cape Horn. The company had the right to mint money, build and maintain armies and forts, forge alliances with foreign powers, acquire territory, declare war, arrange peace treaties and take justice into their own hands when lawbreakers required punishment.

For about sixty years, the company traded in various Oriental goods, but the emphasis shifted when King Charles II married the tea-loving Portuguese princess, Catherine of Braganza. Once she had taught the English aristocracy also to develop a taste for the expensive Chinese herb, tea became the company's most important commodity.

Modern Taiwanese tea bowls and pots set out on a wooden draining tray ready for the Oolong tea ceremony (*The Tea Council*)

gradually seasons the earthenware so that it enhances the true quality of the tea each time it is brewed. Soaps and detergents should never be used inside such a pot. After use, it should simply be rinsed, inverted and allowed to dry. It is perhaps from this respectful care of Yixing pottery that Western tea-drinkers developed the myth that teapots should never be washed inside. Glazed teapots should be cleaned and well rinsed before re-use, but the interior of Yixing unglazed wares should be allowed to build up a patina that helps make the tea taste more fragrant.

In the very early days of tea-drinking in England, the poet Edmund Waller praised both Queen Catherine and tea in his 'Of Tea Commended by Her Majesty, 1663'. Perhaps he composed this while sipping tea poured from a little redware Chinese teapot.

> Venus her Myrtle, Phoebus has her bays;
> Tea both excels, which she vouchsafe to praise.
> The best of Queens, and best of herbs, we owe
> To that bold nation which the way did show
> To the fair regions where the sun doth rise,
> Whose rich production we so justly prize.
> The Muse's friend, tea doth our fancy aid,
> Repress those vapours which the head invade,
> And keep the palace of the soul serene,
> Fit on her birthday to salute the Queen.

2

porcelain teapots from China and Japan

'In a Porcelain Vessel'

As well as skilfully manufacturing decorative earthenwares, the Chinese craftsmen of the seventeenth century also made the most exquisite porcelain tea wares. The most important and well known of the Chinese potteries were in Jingdezhen in Jiangxi Province in north-eastern China. In *A General Description of China*, 1787, Abbé Grosier wrote: 'Ching-tê Chên [a European transcription of the Chinese name] contains about five hundred furnaces for making porcelain. . . . The flames and clouds of smoke which rise from them in different places, show even at a distance the extent and size of this celebrated village.'

Party in a Courtyard of a House Drinking Tea – one of a set of six in gouache by the Anglo-Chinese School, c. 1790. (National Trust Photographic Library/John Hammond)

In Japan, porcelains were made in the province of Arita and the teapots produced there followed traditional designs from both China and Korea. The decoration almost always used attractive images from the natural world and was executed in strong, bright colours.

When the fine translucent Oriental teapots arrived in the European ports on board the same battered ships that brought the precious tea, those that came across them were entranced by their delicacy, pleasing proportions, neat and narrow spouts and the beauty and clarity of the birds and butterflies, insects and animals, flowers and trees, buildings and human figures that decorated the outer surface. Customers did not seem to mind that the different pieces were not of matching designs. They were delighted simply to own some of these perfectly formed vessels and to display them on shelves in their closets alongside the jars that held the tea.

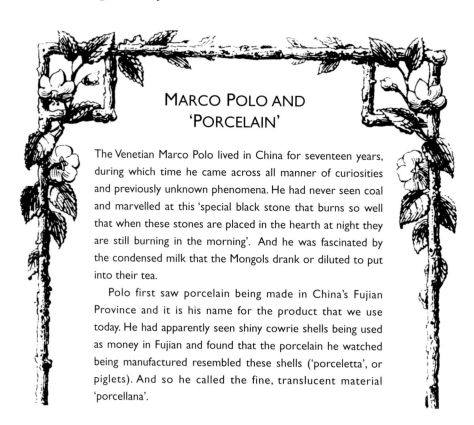

MARCO POLO AND 'PORCELAIN'

The Venetian Marco Polo lived in China for seventeen years, during which time he came across all manner of curiosities and previously unknown phenomena. He had never seen coal and marvelled at this 'special black stone that burns so well that when these stones are placed in the hearth at night they are still burning in the morning'. And he was fascinated by the condensed milk that the Mongols drank or diluted to put into their tea.

Polo first saw porcelain being made in China's Fujian Province and it is his name for the product that we use today. He had apparently seen shiny cowrie shells being used as money in Fujian and found that the porcelain he watched being manufactured resembled these shells ('porceletta', or piglets). And so he called the fine, translucent material 'porcellana'.

Tea was such an expensive luxury that the porcelain jars that held the tea, and the pots and bowls, were all kept, often on display, in the closet of the lady or gentleman of the house. The closet was a small reception room next to or very near the bed chamber and it was here that guests were received and entertained. If tea was to be served, the servant's role was to arrange chairs around a small table, place the necessary equipage on the table and fetch hot water from the kitchen. The host or hostess carried out all the other rituals involved in the preparation and serving of the tea.

The Dowager Countess of Dorset, like the Duchess of Lauderdale, started collecting Chinese porcelains in the 1670s and 1680s and an inventory made in November 1682 records that she owned at least 'two tea potts – tipt [decorated with gold]', as well as various dishes, bowls and other pieces of fine china ware. At the Bankes' family home, Kingston Hall, the household accounts show that Mr Bankes

Pay'd for a teapot, 2/9
Pay'd for a China teapot 6/- [in January 1706] . . .
Pay'd for a teapot 1/-, for a cup 6d [in 1707] . . .
Pay'd for two teapots 6/-, for a pair of tongs 7/-
a teapot, dishes and saucers 6/8 [in 1709]

By 1713, Margaret Bankes had acquired nine teapots, while, in 1710, the records of William Blathwayt of Dyrham Park in Gloucestershire reveal that he owned '5 Tea Potts, a Tea pott & Canister, 6 China Tea pots & 1 Stone one . . .'.

Many of the tea bowls, pots and jars were in the simple blue-and-white designs favoured by the Chinese potters, and Daniel Defoe suggested that it was Queen Mary's liking for such motifs that led to the English craze for Oriental porcelains in the 1690s. Alongside the clear blue-and-white patterns of the Chinese tea bowls that sat so proudly on closet shelves were also displayed pots and dishes from Yeuzhou (in China's Zhejiang Province), where some of the finest and most famous porcelains were made in a blue-green, jade-like finish. The seventeenth-century Chinese poet Xu Xin made sure that the world would remember these fine pieces by describing them in his poem 'The Secret-Colour Porcelain Teacup Left Behind from the Tribute':

> Blend green and blue into a refreshing hue,
> We offer new porcelain as tribute to the throne;
> The cups cleverly fashioned like the full moon softened by spring water,
> Light as thin ice, setting off the green tea
> Like an ancient mirror and dappled moss on a table,
> Like dewy budding lotus blooms bidding the lake farewell,
> Green as the fresh brew of Zhongshan's bamboo leaves.
> How can I drink my fill, ill and frail as I am?

Thomas Smith and his Family at Upton House, Warwickshire, 1733, by Robert West. As in so many family portraits of the period, the tea table provides the focal point of the composition, highlighting the family's wealth and elegance. (*National Trust Photographic Library*)

Chinese porcelain teapot made for the export market in the mid-eighteenth century and decorated with flowers imitating the style used by Meissen and other European potteries at the time. (*John Pearman*)

'With tea came the China-ware to drink it out of. The Company [The East India Company] did not itself import China-ware, so that it was a monopoly enjoyed by the officers, and not reckoned as part of their allowance of space in the ship. China ware came in boxes, not to exceed thirteen inches in height, which were disposed of so as to form a flooring for the tea.'
D.C. Northcote Parkinson, *Trade in the Eastern Seas 1793–1813*, 1937

With a growing trade in Oriental table wares, the English language adopted the name of the country to denote all porcelain dishes, bowls, pots and plates. The word appeared as cheyney, cheney, chyna, chenea and chiney until it eventually settled as 'china'. In October 1686, the East India Company wrote to the agent in charge of their station at Fort St George in Madras with the following instruction: '. . . we give you leave for the future, if you like the proposition, to send us any entire cargo of chyna goods proper for Europe markets . . .'.

At first, European tea-drinkers were happy to buy their teapots from the odd mix of assorted pieces that arrived in the Dutch, Portuguese, French and English ports. But soon, the wealthy and fashionable learned that they could order personalised items from the Chinese manufacturers and so requested pots with family coats of arms, initials and particular designs. An anonymous American writer explained how the porcelain trade was carried on in China: 'The china-ware is brought from the country (Ching-tê Chên) plain, and painted according to fancy in the city (Canton); they make us pay double price when they put a cipher on it, because they say it must go again into the kiln. They are great copyists and we have several sets of China to order with the family coat of arms.' As well as special designs being made for individuals and families, various associations and religious and political organisations commissioned their own items. These included Jesuits, medical practitioners, London hospitals, trade companies, the Mansion House in London, Freemasons and supporters of the Scottish pretender, Prince Charles Edward Stuart. Motifs ranged from a particular person's initials, European hunting scenes, crests and coats of arms, Masonic symbols and political slogans.

Silver spouts and chains to attach teapot lid to spout were often added in Europe. In April 1711, Sir John Bankes of

While it is unlikely that the first European tea-drinkers had ever heard of seventeenth-century Chinese Emperor Kien Lung, his advice concerning the preparation of tea in a Chinese teapot was very sound:

'Set a teapot over a slow fire; fill it with cold water; boil it long enough to turn a lobster red; pour it on the quantity of tea in a porcelain vessel; allow it to remain on the leaves until the vapour evaporates; then sip it slowly and all your sorrows will follow the vapour.'

THE CHINESE TEA HOUSE

China's tea houses have for centuries been at the centre of the social life of each individual village. In the distant past, they were frequented only by the men of the community and by travelling farmers and salesmen looking for rest and shelter. Today, although gambling, business deals and financial discussions still go on, there is a mixed atmosphere and people flock there to play chess, enjoy the singers and folk artists who perform there regularly and generally take pleasure from a family day out.

Tea is brewed in pots or directly in bowls, mugs or glasses, depending on the region, and waiters move from table to table carrying a long-spouted copper kettle of boiling water to offer refills. These men are highly skilled at balancing their trays of cups and bowls, and at pouring exactly the right amount of water into each pot or bowl for the perfect infusion.

Kingston Hall paid 3*s* and 6*d* for a 'silver spout for a teapot'. An inventory from 1688 for Burghley House detailed that a mantelshelf garniture for the closet of Ann, Countess of Exeter, included '1 brown & white relev'd tea pott with gilt handle, spout top and bottoms and a little figure and chaines on the top of it, 1 white tea pott and cover, guilt spout and chaine on it'.

By the early 1700s, tea-drinking was an important part of daily social life among the upper classes and the teapot was an indispensable piece of household equipment. Poet Duncan Campbell recognised the importance of tea to all self-respecting upper-class ladies when he composed 'A Poem upon Tea' in 1735:

Teapot from an Edwardian breakfast teaset for one.

Part of an armorial tea servic[e]
Stourhead, Wiltshire. Such po[rcelain]
wares were decorated either [to]
order in China or in Europe a[fter]
importation from China.
(*National Trust Photographic Library/John Bethell*)

I would not keep you, ladies from your TEA,
Of more Importance your Affairs may be.
The following POEM truly was design'd!
For th'Entertainment of the Female-kind.

Sirs, Let the Praises of the Fair
Employ your Tongues, and please your Ear;
How insipid wou'd this World be,
Without some female Love, and Tea:

* * *

Tea is the sparkling Subject of my Song,
Come, fairer Sex, and listen to my Tongue:
For what you love so dearly, I defend,
And thus its Virtues to the World commend . . .

Chinese porcelain export ware from the second
half of the eighteenth century, hand-painted with a
design that echoes the type used on European
teapots of the period. (*John Pearman*)

3

earthenware teapots from Europe and North America

'In Imitation and as Curious'

As Chinese red earthenware pots gained in popularity, so the English potters made their first attempts to copy them in local clay. As one of the first of two European countries (with Portugal) to start importing tea and tea wares from the Orient, Holland played a key role in the creation of European table wares.

The trade in pottery teapots in Europe had its origins in the manufacture of earthenwares on the Spanish island of Majorca. This enamel-glazed pottery was copied and developed into 'majolica' in Italy, 'faience' in France and tin-glazed 'Delftware' in Holland. When the Ming Dynasty fell in 1644, there was an interruption to the traffic of tea and porcelains between Holland and China and so, to breach the gap, the Dutch potteries expanded

Pottery American teapot decorated with silver chains and ornate lettering. This special-order pot has a pottery infuser inside that sits the full depth of the pot and allows plenty of room for brewing. (*John Pearman*)

17

production to meet the continued demand. Consumers throughout Europe now had the opportunity of owning authentic Chinese wares, Italian Majolica, imitations of the Italian wares made in Holland, proper Delftware and cheaper lead-glazed Dutch earthenwares.

In England the term Delftware was used to describe shiny, white pottery that was decorated with brightly coloured, rather simplistic designs in clear blue, green, red, yellow or purple. Some potteries produced these while others concentrated on copying the Chinese redwares. Celia Fiennes described in her travel diary, *The Journeys of Celia Fiennes in 1698*, how she '. . . went to this Newcastle in Staffordshire to see them making the fine tea-potts cups and saucers of the fine red earth, in imitation and as curious as that which comes from China'.

In 1777, Josiah Wedgwood told in a letter how the Elers brothers, who left their native Holland in the 1680s to settle first in Vauxhall and then in Staffordshire in 1693, had played a key role in developing the early European and British techniques: 'The next improvement introduced by Mr Elers was the refining of our common red clay by sifting and making it into Tea and Coffee ware in imitation of Chinese Red porcelaine [the Chinese pots were called red porcelain] by casting it in plaster moulds, and turning it on the outside upon lathes, and ornamenting it with the Tea branch in relief in imitation of the Chinese manner of ornamenting this ware' (reproduced from *Wedgwood's Letters to Bentley, 1772–1780*, London, The Woman's Printing Society Ltd, 1903). Pots by the Elers brothers, with their unglazed outer surface and raised decoration, continued to be extremely popular throughout the first fifty years of the eighteenth century.

In the mid-nineteenth century, William Makepeace Thackeray recognised the importance of the teapot in England and wrote in *Pendennis* (c. 1848):
'What part of confidante has that poor teapot played ever since the kindly plant was introduced among us. Why myriads of women have cried over it, to be sure! What sickbeds it has smoked by! What fevered lips have received refreshment from it! Nature meant very kindly by women when she made the tea plant; and with a little thought, what series of pictures and groups the fancy may conjure up and assemble round the teapot and sup.'

However, the pots made in Europe were not generally considered to match the fine quality of the Oriental pots and, in 1753, Nicholas Crisp wrote in the *Public Advertiser*, '. . . the porcelain ware of China is free from these imperfections, and is on this account become of such general use, that it must be considered as a great Acquisition to this Nation, could a domestic Manufacture be introduced, that might supply the place of this foreign Commodity'.

The first major producer of fine English stonewares in England was John Dwight (1672–1703) of Fulham, and similar teapots were subsequently made at Burslem in Staffordshire by John Astbury and Josiah Twyford and in Nottinghamshire by Morleys of Mughouse Lane and others. As tea-drinking grew in popularity, Dwight and other English and European potters worked to perfect their skill in copying the Chinese originals. At his Staffordshire factory, Thomas Whieldon (1719–95) invented what he called 'solid agate', which layered clays of different colours and gave a marbled effect to the appearance of the pot. The salt-glaze, which gave a hard, thick, slightly pitted finish, came into its own in the 1740s and 1750s and resulted in several of the major factories producing thousands of square, round, octagonal, hexagonal and fantasy pots in the shape of houses, seashells, camels, bears and other animals.

Wedgwood himself, a pivotal member of the English school of pottery, was still manufacturing such 'red teapots' for both the domestic and export market

One of Wedgwood's famous vegetable teapots dating from the middle of the eighteenth century. *(Image by Courtesy of the Wedgwood Museum Trust Limited, Barlaston, England)*

Frontispiece from Jonas Hanway's *A Journal of Eight Day's Journey to which is Added an Essay on Tea*, published in 1757. Hanway remarked upon the fact that at the beginning of the eighteenth century, 'The use of tea descended to the Plebœan order amongst us'.

towards the end of the eighteenth century. He also worked in solid agate and wrote in his experiment book, '. . . about the beginning of 1759 – I had already made an imitation of Agate which was esteemed beautiful and made a considerable improvement, but people were surfeited with wares of these various colours'. However, it was Wedgwood's creamwares that allowed the large-scale production of affordable teapots and brought him fame. For this he added calcinated flint to the clay and fired it at a higher temperature, which gave the teapots a lighter but more durable quality. In partnership with Thomas Whieldon, Wedgwood produced creamware teapots in the shape of cauliflowers, melons, pineapples, cabbages and other fruits and vegetables and he took the sensible step of asking his wife to test his designs before they were produced commercially. Wedgwood wrote in a letter to a customer in 1767: 'I can serve you the cream color teapots of 12 to 24 to the doz. . . . I will sell them to you at Warehouse price at 3s 6d each . . .'.* When Queen Charlotte

---

* '12 to 24'. This is a potter's dozen connected with the volume of the vessel. There are twelve pint pots to the dozen, and twenty-four smaller ones to the dozen.

The Wedgwood works at Etruria, officially opened by Josiah Wedgwood on 13 June 1769. *(Image by Courtesy of the Wedgwood Museum Trust Limited, Barlaston, England)*

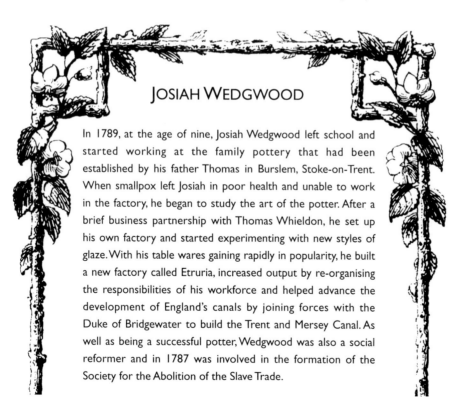

JOSIAH WEDGWOOD

In 1789, at the age of nine, Josiah Wedgwood left school and started working at the family pottery that had been established by his father Thomas in Burslem, Stoke-on-Trent. When smallpox left Josiah in poor health and unable to work in the factory, he began to study the art of the potter. After a brief business partnership with Thomas Whieldon, he set up his own factory and started experimenting with new styles of glaze. With his table wares gaining rapidly in popularity, he built a new factory called Etruria, increased output by re-organising the responsibilities of his workforce and helped advance the development of England's canals by joining forces with the Duke of Bridgewater to build the Trent and Mersey Canal. As well as being a successful potter, Wedgwood was also a social reformer and in 1787 was involved in the formation of the Society for the Abolition of the Slave Trade.

ordered an entire creamware service from Wedgwood, she was so delighted with it that she arranged for it to be re-named Queen's Ware.

In 1806 the Spode works in Stoke-on-Trent also achieved a royal warrant (the first of six) when George, the Prince of Wales visited the factory. A few years later, as George IV, he visited Spode again with his queen, Caroline, who purchased a service of 'fine stone china' from the Staffordshire warehouse.

From 1800 to 1820, a number of new factories started producing 'dry-bodies' stoneware teapots in caneware, redware, white vitreous stoneware and black basalt. The majority of these pots had an oval form, a curved spout and decorative moulding around the outside, often in panels divided by frames of foliage, flowers and classical scrolling. An ornate rim stood proud around the lid and the latter's finial was often formed as a hoop, a swan, a fish, a Chinese figure or a fleur-de-lis. Pots made in black basalt were particularly popular as they contrasted very effectively with the pure whiteness of a lady's hand and arm as she poured the tea.

In the New World, migrant potters developed the skills and trades they had taken with them from Europe, and earthenware teapots were produced in great numbers, while more were shipped in from England. American potteries manufactured principally earthenware and stoneware pots, and Vermont became an important centre because deposits of the right sort of clay were

The Hook Cover Teapot by the Hall China Company, USA, first made in 1940 and produced throughout that decade. (*Hall China Company*)

HALL CHINA COMPANY

Established in 1903 in East Liverpool, Ohio, USA, the Hall China Company became one of the most influential teapot manufacturers in North America. After a shaky start, the company developed a glaze that allowed single firing and a finished pot that would not craze. The hard, non-porous pieces that the factory produced were so successful that when the First World War broke out in 1914 and cut off the regular supply of table and cooking wares from Europe, Hall benefited from demands from the home market. In 1919, with its new line in gold-decorated teapots, the company ran a campaign to teach Americans how to brew tea correctly and became the USA's largest manufacturer of decorated teapots. Today, the Hall China Company have a teapot collectors' page on their website, which gives information about Hall's teapots and designs, collecting teapots, their history, tea books and relevant events.

discovered there. Ohio, too, was found to have suitable clay and many new factories sprang up in the area, including the Hall China Company, which became one of the USA's most famous teapot manufacturers.

If porcelains were too expensive for the majority of tea-drinkers in North America, Europe and Britain, stonewares and earthenwares were accessible to those with a tighter budget and, by the beginning of the nineteenth century, every household had some form of teapot warming on the hearth, dispensing tea at the kitchen table or on display on shelves and in cupboards.

Many people around the world today have treasured collections of teapots and it seems that the hobby is not a new one. In his *Cantor Lectures*, published in 1890, Richard Banister included a chapter on the 'Collection of Teapots', a hobby that by the end of the nineteenth century appears to have become quite a craze. He wrote: 'The round-the-world traveller . . . brings one or more teapots if she brings anything from the Far East. Teapot collectors are now

The Aladdin Teapot by the Hall China Company, USA, introduced in 1939 and produced into the 1970s. (*Hall China Company*)

'To a European, the [tea] ceremony is lengthy and meaningless. When witnessed more than once, it becomes intolerably monotonous. . . . But it is not for him that the tea ceremonies were made. If they amuse those for whom they were made, they amuse them, and there is nothing more to be said. In any case, tea ceremonies are perfectly harmless . . .'
Basil Hall Chamberlain (1849–1912), *Japanese Things*, 1891

Majolica glazed cockerel teapot made by Minton in 1877. The love of novelty shapes was inherited from the Chinese and has inspired the design of pots ever since. (*Minton Archives, Royal Doulton plc*)

learned from the Persians to the Coreans, and the Coreans passed it on to the Japanese. The Chinese and the Japanese adapted and modified the Persian ideas, but the Coreans have followed them closely to modern times, and Persian forms and decorations are conspicuous in all their best work. The Corean teapot illustrated by M. Jacquemart in his great work on the ceramic art is the same in lines and ornament as his Persian pieces.

OWARI.

The constant and more common use of the teapot in the household led toward a lower and broader vase or body for the vessel, and

MIKAWA.

the opening at the top, or cover, kept enlarging in diameter until there have been reached those Chinese teapots whose spouts and handles alone save them from being covered cups. The covered bowls or cups in which the leaves are steeped and brought to one in the great shops, the tea gardens and yaamens of China, are survivals of the earthen bowls in which the very first infusions of the medicinal leaf were made ; but their use today is to convey the sense of individual and absolute possession to the drinker, and to prevent the waste of any of the costly teas used at such places.

Aside from the artistic and intrinsic value of any of the specimens, a collection of teapots has a warmer and more personal interest than a collection of almost any other article of household use

or ornament could have, and appeals to one's domestic and hospitable thoughts. Sentiment and fancy enshrine the teapot, and poets and philosophers have immortalized it. It has associations particularly human, and the sight of a plump round body with a spout and handle suggests cheery home scenes, inspiring hospitalities, reviving energies and an atmosphere of hope and kindliness. A collector has a special delight in handling and

KIOTO.

even using them, and the woman collector rejoices herself and redeems her pieces from the reproach of uselessness by chris-

OLD SATSUMA.

tening them all from time to time before the afternoon altar of society, the tea-table.

A page from Richard Banister's *Cantor Lectures on Sugar, Coffee, Tea, and Cocoa: Their Origin, Preparation, and Uses*, 1890, essential reading for anyone interested at the time in teapots from the Orient.

By depressing the plunger in the lid of Royle's inventive teapot, the lady of the house could, without any effort at all, dispense exactly one cup of tea.

nearly as numerous in the great circling army of globe-trotters as are amateur photographers. . . . If such collections could be made chronologically complete, the rude and primitive earthenware pots in which tea was first made, and the graceful and artistic creations of this century would show the extremist contrasts of evolution.' Banister recognises the enjoyment to be had in collecting such items and told his readers: 'A collector has a special delight in handling and even using them, and the woman collector rejoices herself and redeems her pieces from the reproach of uselessness by christening them all from time to time before the afternoon altar of society, the tea-table.'

During the later years of the nineteenth century, 'inventive' or 'novelty' teapots were created by several of the major potteries. Double-chambered and double-spouted teapots allowed hostesses to brew two different sorts of tea in one pot, 'The Simple Yet Perfect' teapot was tipped up at 90 degrees to separate leaves from infusion, and Royle's 'self-pouring' pot allowed one cup of tea to be dispensed by the simple depression of a plunger without the pot having to be lifted from the table. Pots formed as caricatures of political figures, as elephants, crinoline ladies, monkeys, motor cars, cottages, Humpty Dumpty and Chinamen, delighted the tea-consuming public then and continue to do so today.

porcelain teapots from Europe and North America

'Little Inferior to those

from China'

During the second half of the seventeenth century, European potters struggled to emulate the Chinese in their manufacture of fine porcelain and only managed to produce a type of earthenware coated with an opaque, enamel-like glaze. Stoneware pots, produced a little later, were of inferior quality to the Chinese wares and did not withstand the heat of boiling water. At St Cloud, the French managed to create a soft-paste (or artificial) porcelain in the late seventeenth century, but it was not until 1709 that two Germans discovered, quite by chance, that the secret ingredient was kaolin clay (also known as china clay). Johann-Friedrich Boettger, a druggist and alchemist, and E.W. Tshirnhaus, also an alchemist, found that the addition of kaolin to the clay mixture allowed them to make a true hard-paste porcelain. In Europe, new hard-paste porcelain works were established at Meissen in Germany and at Chantilly, Vincennes and Sèvres in France. These factories started producing wonderfully fine wares for the royal courts and for other wealthy customers, often mimicking the Chinese style and often using Oriental-style white-and-

Interior with Three Figures by Dutch artist Josef Laurens Dyckmans (1811–88). While sitting drinking tea from her porcelain tea wares, an elderly lady is offered some fruit by her granddaughter. (*Courtesy of the Trustees of the V&A*)

Below, opposite: A cube-shaped teaset by Minton, designed originally for use on ocean-going liners. (*Minton Archives, Royal Doulton plc*)

blue decoration. Sometimes the pots were even given false Chinese markings on the unglazed underside to try to fool prospective buyers that they were not European at all.

The majority of tea wares made in England during the eighteenth century were of soft-paste not hard-paste porcelain, and included a glass compound mixed with the clay. Although this gave a reasonably hard substance, pieces often lost their shape during firing. English soft-paste porcelain-ware factories were established at Chelsea, Derby, Longton Hall, Worcester, Liverpool, Lowestoft and Bow. In his *Tour of Great Britain*, published in 1748, Daniel Defoe reported: 'The first village we come to is Bow: where a large manufactory of Porcelaine is lately set up. They have already made large quantities of Tea-cups, saucers, etc which by some skilful persons are said to be little inferior to those brought from China.' Sadly, the only potteries to survive from that group of early soft-paste manufacturers were Worcester and Derby.

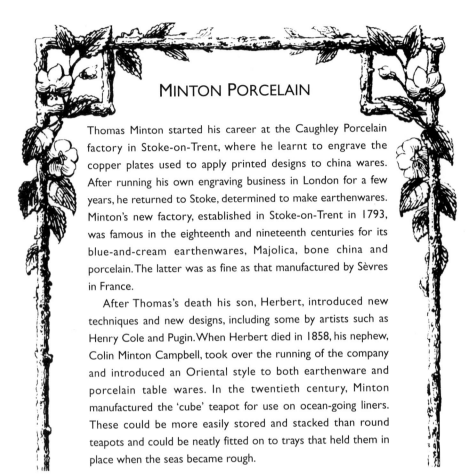

MINTON PORCELAIN

Thomas Minton started his career at the Caughley Porcelain factory in Stoke-on-Trent, where he learnt to engrave the copper plates used to apply printed designs to china wares. After running his own engraving business in London for a few years, he returned to Stoke, determined to make earthenwares. Minton's new factory, established in Stoke-on-Trent in 1793, was famous in the eighteenth and nineteenth centuries for its blue-and-cream earthenwares, Majolica, bone china and porcelain. The latter was as fine as that manufactured by Sèvres in France.

After Thomas's death his son, Herbert, introduced new techniques and new designs, including some by artists such as Henry Cole and Pugin. When Herbert died in 1858, his nephew, Colin Minton Campbell, took over the running of the company and introduced an Oriental style to both earthenware and porcelain table wares. In the twentieth century, Minton manufactured the 'cube' teapot for use on ocean-going liners. These could be more easily stored and stacked than round teapots and could be neatly fitted on to trays that held them in place when the seas became rough.

In 1800 the English potter Josiah Spode, who served his apprenticeship with Thomas Whieldon, is credited with the invention of 'bone china', which added bone ash, flint and feldspar to clay to give a fine, hard, translucent china. In 1798 bone china was introduced at the Minton works in Stoke-on-Trent, and the factory produced tea bowls without handles, teacups with handles and three sizes of teapot in a variety of shapes – round, oval, fluted and square. From 1800 until 1816, the first of Minton's pattern books offered 140 possible designs and these catalogues were distributed to retailers so that clients could choose from the pretty two-dimensional water-colour drawings of tea bowls and saucers. The finished goods reached their new owner a few weeks later.

More and more households owned collections of tea wares from China and Japan, from Europe and England and, during his visit to England in 1784, the French traveller and writer François de la Rochefoucauld commented upon the importance of the teapot and other tea equipage to the prestige of the typical English family in *A Frenchman in England*: 'Throughout the whole of England the drinking of tea is general. . . . It provides the rich with an opportunity to display their magnificence in the matter of tea-pots, cups, and so on, which are always of most elegant design based upon Etruscan and other models of antiquity.'

Each hostess sat like a queen over her teapot, holding court just as Catherine of Braganza must have done in the seventeenth century when introducing the new herb to her friends. Those in attendance at such gatherings had to wait for the lady of the house to pour the tea and favour them with a little bowlful. Alexander Boswell of Auchinlech describes such a scene in *Edinburgh or the Ancient Royalty, A Sketch of Former Manners*, 1810:

A lady decides which design of teapot suits her best. (*Twinings*)

30

Hapless the wight who, with lavish sup,
Empties too soon the Lilliputian cup!
Tho' patience fails, and tho' with thirst he urns,
All, all must wait till the last cup returns.
That cup returned now see the hostess ply
The Tea-pot, measuring with equal eye,
To all again, at once she grants her boon,
Dispensing her gunpowder by platoon . . .

In the USA, potters also tried to copy the hard porcelain of the Chinese potters, but it was not until Andrew Duché: discovered the right type of clay 'on the back of Virginia' (as noted by the *Public Advertiser* in 1753) that the manufacture of American porcelain was possible. English potter William Cookworthy wrote of Duché: '. . . he discovered both the petunze [china stone] and kaolin [china clay]. It is this latter earth which he says is essential to the success of the manufacture.'

The ritual of brewing and serving tea was steeped in the manners and etiquette of elegant society, but these, of course, varied from country to country. After a visit to France in 1775, Dr Johnson was shocked by the lack of what he considered proper manners among the French when it came to the handling of the teapot: 'At Madame [du Boccage's] a literary lady of rank, the footman took the sugar in his fingers and threw it into my coffee. I was going to put it aside; but hearing it was made on purpose for me, I e'en tasted Tom's fingers. The same lady must needs make tea à l'anglaise. The spout of the teapot did not pour freely; she bade the footman blow into it. France is worse than Scotland for everything except climate.' Surely in Britain, any footman or butler caught blowing down the spout of a teapot would have been instantly dismissed.

All servants had to know exactly how to prepare the room for tea and

'And in the drowsy land of Afternoon,
When time hangs heavy and the spirits droop,
Bring me a little tray, a little spoon
A little teapot (with a decent 'stroup'),
A little sugar, and a little cream,
A little drop o' tea – and let me dream.'
Aquilo, 'A Drop o'Tea', 1926

Veilleuse, designed in three parts to keep the tea warm in the pot. The central chimney lifts off the base to allow the positioning of a candle or spirit burner. The porcelain is decorated with hand-painted views of the Bay of Naples and the eruption of Mount Vesuvius. The light from the burner shines through the translucent porcelain, illuminating the entire scene. (John Pearman)

lay out the relevant items. It was also crucial that they were familiar with how to behave during a tea-drinking gathering and what might be required by guests. In 1823, in *The Footman's Directory, and Butler's Remembrancer*, Thomas Cosnett instructed servants to 'have a teapot on a tray with hot water in it, in case any of the ladies' tea should be too strong'. So teapots sometimes served as hot water jugs as well as brewing vessels.

At the end of the eighteenth century, the popular round body of the teapot gave way to an oval plan, which in the later 1800s became more of a rectangle. Bodies of pots were sometimes squat and bulbous, sometimes taller and somewhat ostentatious. Through the nineteenth century, the major porcelain factories in Europe and Britain produced thousands of teapots that followed the trends of the time – from Adams-style Classicism to Rococo exuberance. Towards the end of the nineteenth century, the English Aesthetic movement

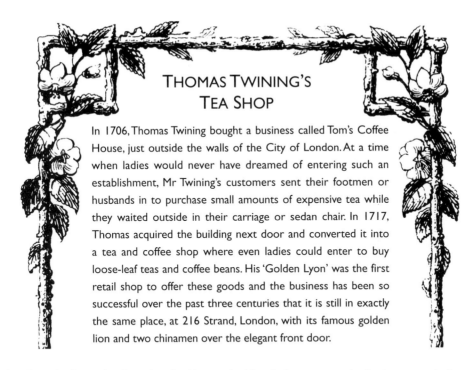

THOMAS TWINING'S TEA SHOP

In 1706, Thomas Twining bought a business called Tom's Coffee House, just outside the walls of the City of London. At a time when ladies would never have dreamed of entering such an establishment, Mr Twining's customers sent their footmen or husbands in to purchase small amounts of expensive tea while they waited outside in their carriage or sedan chair. In 1717, Thomas acquired the building next door and converted it into a tea and coffee shop where even ladies could enter to buy loose-leaf teas and coffee beans. His 'Golden Lyon' was the first retail shop to offer these goods and the business has been so successful over the past three centuries that it is still in exactly the same place, at 216 Strand, London, with its famous golden lion and two chinamen over the elegant front door.

A hand-worked sampler featuring the blue-and-white designs so popular for tea wares in the second half of the nineteenth century. (*National Trust Photographic Library*)

Edwardian advertisement for Co-operative Tea being brewed here in a giant earthenware teapot. (*Author's Collection*)

developed a fondness for blue-and-white porcelains and a number of teapots were once again made in the Oriental style.

As tea gradually became cheaper and worked its way down the social ladder, there was at least one teapot in every stately home, every upper-class mansion, every modest middle-class suburban house and every country cottage. The drinking of tea had become central to society, as David Elliston's quotation reveals: 'The making of tea is one of the most deep-seated British rituals, impervious to change, so the apparent lineal descent of two-fifths of all teapots in the country from the ancient semi-sacred pot on the hearth – perhaps even going back to the prized cauldrons of the bronze age – is only fitting.'

'Cups! I don't count by cups. I count by pots.' – Wordsworth's scornful reply when asked how many cups of tea he drank.

5

silver teapots

'The Best Silver'

The first ever silver teapot made in England was a gift to the East India Company from George, Lord Berkeley. It bears the inscription 'This silver tea Pott was presented to the Com^ttee of the East India Company by the Right Hon° George Ld Berkeley of Berkeley Castle. A member of that Honourable and worthy Society and A true hearty Lover of them. 1670.' The early manufacture of silver wares was a hard task for the silversmith, for a solid silver ingot had to be reduced by hammering to the thickness required for the teapot being made. Pieces the correct size were then cut from the flattened sheets, the body of the pot was smoothed and feet, handles and spouts were soldered on.

With the invention of a metal rolling mill in the late 1600s, production of silver table wares became easier, quicker and therefore cheaper. George Berkeley's gift to his company was typical in shape for the period, resembling as it did a tall coffee or chocolate pot. Two other early silver teapots from 1670 and a third from 1685 are squat and round, rather like a cantaloup melon. They stand no more than 6 in high, and were probably copies of the small Chinese earthenware pots that were appearing in Europe at the time.

By the beginning of the eighteenth century, silver pots were pear-shaped, round or octagonal and the ends of the elegantly curving spout often took the

Silver teapot by Henry Chawner of London of typical oval shape with matching stand, 1795.
(*J. & S. Stodel*)

form of a bird's head. The lid was hinged, the finial was usually of metal or beautifully polished wood and the handle was also carved in wood or plain wood covered with leather. As the fashion for milk developed at this time, the first silver tea services included little jugs for milk or cream and a matching sugar basin.

Between the 1690s and 1750, George Booth, Earl of Warrington, purchased a good deal of silver tea ware for his home at Dunham Massey. His household inventory lists: 'four teapots with waiters – 2 for Bohea [black tea] with lamp stands, a pot for hot water to the tea tables'. The reference to lamp stands for Bohea is explained by the fact that black China tea can withstand being kept hot in this way, while green tea can become extremely bitter. Booth also owned silver tea canisters, strainer spoons, tongs and 'boats to hold the teaspoons'.

In 1707, the young 2nd Duke Wriothesley, a member of the Bedford family and always very fashionable, had a silver teapot bought for his use and engraved with his coat of arms. It was purchased from David Willaume (known as Gillhomme by the Duke), as his household accounts show:

Monsieur Gillhomme's bill
Livre par D Willaume, Orfèvre
27 avril 1707 Un pot à thé   £14 19s 7d
Facon   £4 2s 6d
Gravure   7s 6d

        £19 9s 7d

Between 1725 and 1750, the pear shape gave way to a global or bullet-shaped body and the French Rococo style greatly influenced the design of

TEA FOR SALE

The names by which teas were sold 350 years ago in Europe and England were very different from those used today. Customers could buy black or green and the most common terms were Bohea, Congo, Souchong and Pekoe for black tea, and Hyson, Singlo and Gunpowder for green varieties. The names developed from Chinese terms for the different leaves or the different methods of manufacture. Bohea is a corruption of 'wu-i', the mountains in Fukien where the tea came from. Congo is derived from 'kong-fu', meaning made with great skill. Souchong simply developed from 'siau-chung', young plant. Pekoe alludes to the little silver hairs on the underside of the young Chinese leaves. Hyson comes from 'yu-tsien', which means before the rains, so referred to young green teas. Singlo is the name of a range of mountains where high-quality tea was cultivated. And tightly rolled pellets of Gunpowder tea look exactly like the explosive.

Georgian silver tea set dating from about 1824. (*The Tea Council*)

teapots, introducing elaborately decorative flowers, scrolls and spouts like swirling dragons. In the 1770s, the neo-classical style led to straight-sided pots with circular, oval or polygonal bases and vertical sides.

In 1742, Thomas Boulsover accidentally discovered a way of manufacturing 'fused' silver plate. He found that molten silver amalgamated very easily with other metals, especially copper, and, once the technique had been perfected, 'Old Sheffield Plate' and 'Fused Plate' (one and the same thing) allowed the cheaper production of silver table wares for those who could not afford solid silver. In the 1850s, 'fused' silver pots were replaced by electroplated pots. Tea had by now become very popular among the middle classes, who craved beautiful tea wares. However, these groups were unable to afford the prices paid by the aristocracy and other wealthier members of society for solid silver pots.

Solid or plated, a silver pot needed careful handling by the servants. Thomas Cosnett's *The Footman's Directory, and Butler's Remembrancer* of 1823 included the following instructions:

The Tea-pot you must be very particular in wiping, so that none of the tea-leaves shall be left in the pot: if it is silver, let the inside be wiped dry, and handle it lightly, as the handle of the teapot is easily broken off: if the spout of the tea-pot gets furred up, have a small piece of wire or wood to push up and down it, but be careful not to break the grate of it in so doing . . . if the tea-pot is not in constant use, let it be wiped dry and the lid left open, or filled full of clean paper, or otherwise it will soon get musty.

In North America, the demand for tea silvers came from Boston, New York and Philadelphia — all wealthy towns where tea-drinking was well established. American craftsmen copied English shapes and styles, believing that English influence in all aspects of social and cultural life was most important.

At the turn of the eighteenth century, silver tea services began to appear in North America. In about 1792, silversmith Paul Revere made a set of tea equipage for John Templeman of Boston that included a teapot with stand on four feet, a cream jug and a sugar urn. (This is still in the keeping of the Minneapolis Institute of Art.) In Britain at this time, a full tea set included teapot, warming stand, milk or cream jug, sugar bowl or basin, coffee pot, tray, tea caddy, caddy spoon, teaspoons, sugar tongs and tea strainer.

Many people did not own a matching tea set, simply because they could not afford to order all the pieces at the same time. Silver teaspoons and sugar tongs may have been in the family already and it was sometimes possible to afford a silver pot, while a little milk jug or sugar basin might be added later. In *The Private Life of a Country House, 1912–1939* (1980), Lesley Lewis recalls family tea times when she was a young girl at the beginning of the twentieth century:

An oval mahogany tray, with a shell centre in marquetry and brass handles, was set in front of my mother's place and on this were a reproduction Georgian silver teapot, an Irish silver sugar bowl and milk jug on little

'So here's a toast to the queen of plants,
The queen of plants – Bohea!
Good wife, ring for your maiden aunts,
We'll all have cups of tea.'
Arthur Gray, 'O Tea', 1903

legs, the china slop bowl belonging to the tea-set and the cups and saucers ready for filling and distributing. Hot water was provided by a big silver tea-kettle, a Victorian copy of an eighteenth century design but so long used and polished that it had acquired the delicacy of an antique.

Throughout the nineteenth century, ladies did their very best to make sure that their tea party was as beautifully presented and as stylish as those given by their friends and acquaintances. Etiquette books were invaluable in giving careful instructions as to how to lay out the silver or porcelain teapot and other tea things properly. Marie Bayard included typical information in her *Hints on*

Alfred Dryden Taking Tea in the Hall by Clara Dryden, 1911, hanging in the Great Hall at Canons Ashby. The tea tray holds a typical assortment of silver wares, probably acquired at different times from different sources. (*National Trust Photographic Library/John Hammond*)

Georgian ladies take tea in a bower in the garden – a popular social activity in the eighteenth and early nineteenth centuries.

panelled sides were designed by cabinet-makers to contain and surround the entire kettle and lamp.

From the 1730s, designs became much more ornate and followed fashions in terms of shape and style. By 1750, as tea became a little cheaper, and teapots gradually bigger, so tea kettles also became too large and difficult to lift and the new trend resulted in a fashion for the tea urn. Urns stood proudly in the centre of the tea table, needed no lifting and provided a larger quantity of boiling water with less effort. All that the hostess had to do was open a tap on the side of the urn's body to allow the boiling water to flow into the teapot. Sir Richard Hoare purchased such an urn in 1783 and his household accounts recorded:

Bought of John Folghem 81 Fleet Street, Case & Cabinet maker
Oct 7th Neat brown Jappaned Vase Tea Urn with strong silver handles and hoop
    ring £7.7 0
A neat silver plate in front of ditto urn £0 5 0.

The heat needed to boil the water in the urn was generated by allowing burning charcoal to smoulder in the central hollow cylinder of the apparatus. In 1774, John Wadham patented an urn with a cylindrical bar of solid iron inside a copper socket that ran down the centre of the body. The iron was heated to red hot and then inserted into the copper socket. The following extract is from William Cowper's 'The Task', 1783:

'Now stir the fire, and close the shutters fast,
Let fall the curtains, wheel the sofa round,
And while the bubbling and loud hissing urn
Throws up a steamy column, and the cups
That cheer but not inebriate, wait on each
So let us welcome the peaceful evening in.'

THE THINGS THEY SAID ABOUT TEA

During the eighteenth century, tea had its enemies who did their utmost to discourage people from drinking it. An anonymous 'Essay on the Nature, Use and Abuse of Tea in a Letter to a Lady', 1716–87, made the following accusations: 'First that tea may attenuate the Blood to any Degree necessary to the production of any Disease, which may arise from too thin a state of the Blood. Secondly, that Tea may depauperate the Blood, or waste the Spirits, to any Degree necessary to produce any Disease, which may arise from too poor a Blood.' And those who generally approved of the beverage also had warnings to offer the consuming public. The Lady's and Gentleman's Tea Table by Philanthropists, 1818, told readers: 'black tea is very injurious to those who are troubled with coughs, asthmas, and obstructions of the lungs, proceeding from a vicidity of the juices . . . Green tea should not be drunk by those who are troubled with a frequent laborious, tickling or convulsive cough.'

The poet William Cowper wrote to his friend Lady Hesketh asking her to buy him a grand new tea urn – '. . . the one we have at present having never been handsome, and being now old and patched. A parson once, as he walked across the room, pushed it down with his belly, and it never perfectly recovered itself.'

'Tea, though ridiculed by those who are naturally coarse in their nervous sensibilities, or are become so from wine-drinking, and not susceptible of influence from so refined a stimulant, will always be the favoured beverage of the intellectual'.
Thomas De Quincey, *Confessions of an English Opium Eater*, 1822

Both the urn and the kettle continued to play their part at the tea table. The innovation of William Cowper's 'bubbling and loud-hissing urn' in the middle of the eighteenth century was later strongly condemned by Dr Sigmond, who in 1839 quoted the poet and wrote:

Thus sang one of our most admired poets. . . . It is indeed a question amongst the devotees to the tea-table, whether the bubbling urn has been practically an improvement. Upon our habits, it has driven from us the old national kettle, once the pride of the fireside. The urn may be fairly called the offspring of indolence; it has deprived us, too, of many of those felicitous opportunities of which the gallant forefathers of the present race availed themselves to render them amiable in the eyes of the fairer sex.

Tea urns were elegantly vase-shaped with a narrow, stemmed foot and a graceful tap through which the boiling water was delivered into the teapot. Some have suggested that this style of urn was made to contain brewed tea, but it was actually intended solely as a receptacle for hot water for tea-brewing at breakfast or tea time. Manuel Alavarez Espriella's *Letters from England* of 1807 refers to this design of urn: 'The breakfast-table is a cheerful sight . . . Porcelain is ranged on a Japan waiter . . . the hostess sits at the head of the board and opposite her the boiling water smokes and sings in an urn of Etruscan shape.' In *Manners of Modern Society*, 1872, Eliza Cheadle asked readers: 'What more welcome and cheering sight can meet our eye on the return from a long journey or distant excursion, or from a hardly-contested battle on the croquet-lawn than the hissing, steaming urn, the array of cups and saucers, the sociable genial air which the tea table invariably presents?'

For large gatherings and parties, impressive, three-chambered silver tea and coffee urns could provide the two beverages in large quantities. First designed in the 1790s, the apparatus had a central chamber that contained boiling water and was fitted with taps to dispense water into the two side urns. These smaller chambers were for brewing coffee and tea and taps were fitted to these to allow cups to be filled with the chosen drink.

In some households, the silver tea kettle reigned supreme in preference to the urn from the earliest days right through to the twentieth century. For Queen Victoria, the kettle was crucial, as *The Private Life of the Queen by One of Her Majesty's Servants*, 1897, reveals:

Her Majesty has a strong weakness for afternoon tea. From her early days in Scotland, when Brown and the other gillies used to boil the kettle in a sheltered corner of the moors while Her Majesty and the young princesses sketched, the refreshing cup of tea has ever ranked high in the Royal favour. . . . The tea consumed in the Palaces costs four shillings a pound, and the Queen drinks the same as every one else. Whether the Queen helps to boil the kettle herself, or whether it is brought to her ready made, she always loves her tea.

A Chinese tea kettle with matching stand and lamp, by Wang Hing of Hong Kong, c. 1890. Made to a typical British design, it has Oriental decoration – an applied dragon encircling the body and handle, spout and stand formed as bamboo. The advantage of this style of kettle is that it can remain in its cradle while pivoting to pour boiling water into a jug or teapot. (J. & S. Stodel)

This fictional tea party, created as an advertisement by the tea company Horniman's, shows Queen Victoria (right), Florence Nightingale and Prime Minister William Gladstone (seated left) taking tea and toast together. (*The Tea Council*)

In the USA in 1935, *Vogue* published its *Book of Etiquette*, which also advocated the traditional method of brewing tea with all the old-fashioned tea equipage:

> The ideal hot-water kettle is the sort which has its own alcohol lamp beneath it; and if this sort is used, the lamp is lit after the tray is set down, never before, to prevent accidents. The water in the kettle should be as hot as possible, so that the lighting of the flame brings it at once to the boil. . . . When the hot-water kettle has no spirit lamp, the tea should be made in the kitchen, so that boiling water may be poured directly on the tea leaves, and the tray then brought immediately into the drawing room. In this case, the hot-water kettle is really used only to weaken tea for guests who prefer it that way.

A quiet cup of tea in Victorian times. (*Twinings*)

Pauline Dower, writing of her grandparents Sir George and Lady Trevelyan in *Living at Wallington*, 1984, described how, in the early twentieth century, 'Tea was laid out on a low table with a white starched linen and lace cloth. On a large silver tray stood a silver kettle on its own stand with a spirit lamp lit, beneath it, the tea leaves in a silver caddy, and an empty silver teapot standing ready . . .'.

The introduction of electricity to homes at the end of the nineteenth century revolutionised many routine domestic chores and tea-making was no exception. In 1894, Mappin & Webb advertised a tea kettle that was powered by electricity and the promotional material read, 'the fiery untamed steed of earlier days has been so thoroughly broken in by modern genius and enterprise that it has turned out to be the most tractable and steady going domestic animal, whose uses are practically endless'.

Kettles have always had a tendency to sing or hiss as the steam forces its way out of the spout and a Japanese writer by the name of Sanyo composed the following lines in the late eighteenth century:

> The kettle by its singing my attention claimed;
> I beheld 'fish-eye' bubbles like ocean pearls;
> For the past three decades all my tastes it drained,
> Yet there remains a nectar and my content unfurls.

The modern singing kettle was invented in the 1920s and alerted those waiting to brew the tea that the water had reached the correct temperature.

Eighteenth-century kettle stands (on the lower row) designed by Chippendale to protect the kettle burner from draughts.

Since tea has become a low-priced, everyday commodity all over the world, much of the charm of the brewing ceremony has disappeared. People have forgotten many of tea's associations with beautiful table wares, silver kettles, ornate caddies etc. and simply throw a tea bag into a mug in the kitchen. As the brewing operation moved from drawing room to kitchen, Arthur Reade bemoaned the subsequent drop in standards when he wrote in *Tea and Tea Drinking*, 1884:

Once on a time, no confectioner, railway-station, or refreshment-house could rival the home-made brew made under the eye of the mistress of the household, with the kettle on the hob and the ingredients at hand; but now that the good old custom of tea making is considered unladylike, and the manufacture has been handed over to the servants, the great charm of the beverage has virtually departed . . . Indeed it is surprising in how few houses a good cup of tea can be obtained now that it has become unfashionable for the mistress of the establishment not only to preside over her own tea-table, but to have complete sway over that most necessary article, a kettle of boiling water.

7

dishes and bowls

'To Sip the Enlivening Beverage'

Through the hundreds of years of tea-drinking in China, small handleless ceramic bowls were favoured and, during his travels in the East in 1625, Samuel Purchas discovered that 'They use much the powder of a certaine herbe called chia of which they put as much as a Walnut shell may containe, into a dish of Porcelane, and drink it with hot water' (from *Purchas His Pilgrimes*, 1625). The heavier pottery of a thousand years ago and more gradually disappeared from everyday life in the third, fourth and fifth

Dish and saucer from the Nanking cargo, manufactured in the 1750s and rescued from the South China Sea in 1985. (*Twinings*)

centuries AD as the Chinese potteries developed fine translucent porcelain. Colours varied depending on the different regions from blue-green and white to yellow and brown and even black, which was favoured as a wonderful visual contrast to the pale, frothy green of whipped tea during the Song Dynasty (960–1126).

By the time the Europeans had discovered China's tea and porcelain during the Ming Dynasty (1368–1644), the preference among Chinese tea-drinkers was for blue-and-white bowls and, as trade with Europe grew, so the Chinese potters perfected the technique of adding their designs on to the unfired

An eighteenth-century woodblock Japanese print showing a typical elegant porcelain bowl and lacquer-ware saucer. (*Author's Collection*)

clay and then applying the glaze before firing. During the Qing Dynasty (1644–1800) other colours came into use and tea bowls with multi-coloured designs started appearing in European homes. In May 1672, according to her household accounts, the Duchess of Lauderdale paid a bill for andirons and sconces that also included eighteen teacups at a cost of approximately £18. Apparently these dishes travelled with her whenever she left home. She also owned a case made to hold three 'tay' dishes and another to hold twelve.

Japan was also a source of prized porcelains and the records of the East India Company show that a sale held in November 1699 offered the following tea wares:

Good ex Nassau 1697–9 voyage to Amoy

1 v. fine Japan bason	12s
1 do very fine	£1
4 Japan dishes	5s
6 Japan plates	7s
1 Japan bason	10s
6 Japan bowls	6s

A further sale in April 1702 offered:

Goods ex Dorrill 1699–1701 voyage to Amoy

8 nests Jappan bowls	15. 0d each
6 do	8. 0 each
2,500 Jappan tea cups	6d each
2,690 do saucers	
814 Jappan tea cups	1 6d each
330 Jappan tea cups	5d each
340 do saucers	

The dishes were generally small and held only two or three sips of tea. Some, however, were slightly larger and it was this version that eventually acquired a handle and became the teacup.

The Chinese 'zhong' or 'gaiwan' also made its way to Europe but in smaller numbers as most people seemed to favour the little bowl. The zhong is a brewing and drinking vessel with matching lid and saucer and demands a certain amount of adroit manipulation. The cup and saucer are balanced on one hand while the other hand tilts the lid over the top of the cup to restrain the leaves. The tea is sipped through the narrow gap between the angled lid and the rim of the cup.

Europe's potters quickly started copying the Oriental designs and Daniel Defoe remarked in *A Tour Thro' the Whole Island of Great Britain*, 1724–6, upon the fact that the trade in such table wares was growing fast: 'It is impossible that Coffee, Tea and Chocolate can be so advanced in their consumption, without an eminent encrease of those trades that attend them; whence we see the most noble shops in the city taken up with the most valuable utensils of the Tea-Table.' This increase in trade offered profit-making opportunities to the companies importing goods from the East. After a successful sale of porcelain table wares in 1738, the French East India Company wrote that 'The assortment in the sale . . . was about right. This is more or less what is now required: 10 to 12,000 pairs of blue cups. Those received this year were a good shape and colour, 5–6000 pairs polychrome cups, preferably from Japan rather than China, and certainly no larger than the blue one, 3–4000 sugar boxes, 3–400 teapots.'

JAPANESE TEA BOWLS

In the traditional Japanese green-tea ceremony, or 'Cha-no-yu', each piece of equipage holds an important significance, and bowls, pots, wall hangings and vases are chosen with great care to suit each individual occasion. Tea bowls are divided into three classes: Chinese, Korean and Japanese. The original Chinese bowls were specifically designed for tea-drinking, whereas Korean bowls are thought to have developed from rice bowls into the tea bowls used in Japan for roughly the past 1,200 years. Most of the potteries and porcelain factories in Japan were established by Korean migrants in the ninth century AD and Korean style left its mark on Japanese society and tea-drinking rituals.

Korean pottery bowls are much sought after by true tea connoisseurs in Japan. The generous bowls are hand-made, always have an uneven, slightly rough appearance and are pleasingly light and soft to the touch. The thickness of the pottery is crucial – a bowl that is too thick does not become warm enough, while a bowl that is too thin becomes too hot to hold.

English Family at Tea by Richard Collins. This eighteenth-century painting is composed with the family seated around their silver and Oriental porcelain tea wares in order to demonstrate their wealth and status. (*Courtesy of the Trustees of the V&A*)

Smugglers were meanwhile attempting to bring illicit tea and porcelains into Britain and in 1768 the English East India Company held a six-day sale at The Customs House of smuggled goods that had been confiscated by excise men. Two days were given over to the sale of porcelains and, according to company records, 'On the first day, 7000 cups and saucers, 3000 basins, almost 2800 plates, 600 dishes, 500 bowls were auctioned'.

Porcelain goods from both home and abroad were available in the shops and stalls of general merchants, tea dealers, jewellers, glassware and china sellers. An advertisement in Steele's *Spectator*, issue no. 336, in 1712 announced: 'I am, dear Sir, one of the top china-women about town. One calls for a set of tea dishes, another for a basin, a third for my best green tea.' R. Twining's ledgers for sales at the family shop in Devereux Court, Strand, show that at some point between 1715 and 1720 a Mr Warrender of Bath purchased from them a 'Set of china dishes, a diamond ring, 3 pairs of dice'. During Queen Anne's reign (1702–14), it appears that Twining's did not simply sell dry loose-leaf tea and tea wares, but also served dishes of tea to gentlewomen: '. . . tea was sold by the few houses then in the trade at various prices between twenty and thirty shillings per pound, and that ladies of fashion used to flock to Messrs Twining's house in Devereux Court, in order to sip the enlivening beverage in their small China cups . . .'. This was extremely unusual since the Twining's shop was the only establishment where it was acceptable for respectable ladies to sample and buy tea. All the other coffee houses nearby were frequented by men only.

Silver tea dishes were also available, although they were obviously very impractical, since the handle had yet to make an appearance and fingers must have been scorched while holding the rim of the bowl. Nevertheless, the Duchess of Lauderdale, always a leader of fashion, owned a set of eighteen at Ham House in 1672. This was perhaps not a totally new idea, as a certain Richard Cocks, an employee of the East India Company, recorded in his diary how he learnt to drink tea in Java between 1612 and 1623. He wrote of cups made of porcelain or tin but covered with silver plate in which the leaves were infused. His colleague William Eaton also mentioned in his papers 'three silver porringers to drink chaw in'. Perhaps they found the smaller tea bowls too restricting in the quantity they held and so preferred larger silver bowls instead.

Once tea had replaced ale and beer at breakfast time, larger bowls were also used for the consumption of morning tea by some people. In 1781, the Honourable John Byng (Viscount Torrington) wrote, as quoted in

Pattern No. 112 from Minton pattern books dating from about 1800. (*Minton Archives, Royal Doulton plc*)

The Torrington Diaries, ed. B. Andrews, 1954: 'After a complete shaving, and dressing, and drinking two pint basins of tea, I walk'd thro' the town to a stone gazeabout.' Not for him polite little tea dishes – he liked his tea served by the generous bowlful.

With no handle yet in place on the side of bowls, how were the little containers held when tea was being drunk? From paintings, it would appear that there was no set position for the hand, and bowls were held either by fingers placed around the rim, by neatly gripping the small foot on the underside or by placing the thumb under the bowl and the middle finger on the upper rim. Whichever method the drinker chose, it had, of course, to be neat and elegant. Tea-drinking was seen as an opportunity to show off the fine porcelain and, in the case of ladies, the pure, unblemished whiteness of the skin of the forearm. Edward Young reflected these ideas in his poem 'The Love of Fame, the Universal Passion' in about 1725:

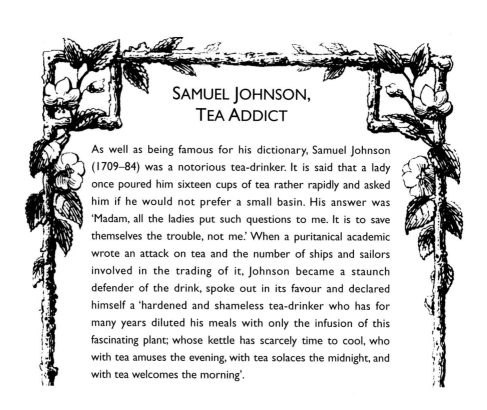

SAMUEL JOHNSON, TEA ADDICT

As well as being famous for his dictionary, Samuel Johnson (1709–84) was a notorious tea-drinker. It is said that a lady once poured him sixteen cups of tea rather rapidly and asked him if he would not prefer a small basin. His answer was 'Madam, all the ladies put such questions to me. It is to save themselves the trouble, not me.' When a puritanical academic wrote an attack on tea and the number of ships and sailors involved in the trading of it, Johnson became a staunch defender of the drink, spoke out in its favour and declared himself a 'hardened and shameless tea-drinker who has for many years diluted his meals with only the infusion of this fascinating plant; whose kettle has scarcely time to cool, who with tea amuses the evening, with tea solaces the midnight, and with tea welcomes the morning'.

Her two red lips affected Zephyrs blow,
To cool the Bohea, and inflame the Beau;
While one white Finger and a Thumb conspire
To lift the Cup and make the World admire.

When guests had drunk enough tea, one way of indicating this was to turn the bowl upside down in the saucer. An anonymous quote from the eighteenth century highlights this important role of the little saucer:

Dear Mrs Hoggins, what? Your cup
Turned in your saucer, bottom up!
Dear me, how soon you've had your fill!

At this stage most people still spoke of a 'dish of tea' rather than a 'cup'. In his poem of 1736, 'In Praise of Tea – A Poem, Dedicated to the Ladies of Great Britain', J.B. Writing Master (a pseudonym) defended those who enjoyed a dish of tea:

When tea was sold for guineas by the pound,
The poor a drinking Tea were never found,
Then only China dishes cou'd be bought
Burnt in with gold, or else in colours wrought:
Now Tee is cheap, so dishes are the same;
Then pray wherein are they so much to blame? . . .

In 1782, the Reverend Woodforde wrote in his diary: 'Mr and Mrs Custance sent us a note this morning, that if we were disengaged, they would drink a dish of Tea with us in the afternoon in a friendly way – I sent a note back that we should be very glad to see them, and about 5 o'clock they came and stayed with us till after 8.' Fanny Burney, likewise, in *The Early Diary of Frances Burney*, wrote on Tuesday, 15 November 1768, 'Monday morning, Mrs Pringle

called here – to invite me to tea in the afternoon . . . we had a charming concert . . . Mr Pringle and Mr Mackenzie came in during the performance, drank a dish of tea . . . and away again'. Dr Samuel Johnson, an avid tea-drinker, certainly enjoyed his dish of tea, as this verse from about 1770 reveals:

> So hear it then, my Rennie dear,
> Nor hear it with a frown;
> You cannot make the tea so fast
> As I can gulp it down.
> I therefore pray thee, Rennie dear,
> That thou wilt give to me
> With cream and sugar softened well,
> Another dish of tea.

Opposite: The Wollaston Family, 1730 by William
Hogarth. This painting shows an evening's
entertainment in a fashionable home – including
card games and tea-drinking. (*Bridgman Art Library*)

'Late blossoms left on the ground,
shoots of bamboo poking up the mud;
the tea bowl, the poem bag –
I took them wherever I went.
My dim dream just taking shape,
Who calls me back to waking?
By the window half in slanting sun
A partridge cries.'
Lu Yu, a Chinese tea-drinker (1125–1209),
'In the Garden: Written at Random'

What about the saucer? Most early paintings show little dishes on which the tea bowls were placed and it is said that the idea of the saucer originated in China when the daughter of a military man found the cups too hot to pass around and so asked a local potter to design a little dish on which the cups could sit. A small circular rim in the centre of the saucer made sure that the dish did not slide around, and so when the porcelain trade started with the West, saucers travelled with the little bowls and became an everyday part of the tea equipage in grand houses.

The design for this tea bowl and saucer, made by
Chamberlain-Worcester in 1801, is often known
as the 'Sir Joshua Reynolds' pattern. (*John Pearman*)

cups and saucers

'How is your Cup'

The gradual evolution from the tea bowl and dish to the cup involved the adaptation of the handle of the English 'posset' cup to the Oriental bowl. Posset cups were used for the consumption of hot beverages made of heated milk, spirits and wines, spices and sugar, and were designed with a handle on each side so that fingers were not burned on the hot earthenware. How sensible, then, to add a little handle to the side of the tea bowl, which had demanded the careful positioning of fingers and thumbs if they were not to feel too much of the heat of the porcelain. Yet, when the European porcelain manufacturers started producing tea wares, they made bowls with handles and bowls without handles and this continued well into the nineteenth century. And without handles they were often referred to as cups as well as dishes, and with handles they were referred to as dishes as well as cups.

There was, however, always a clear distinction between coffee cups and teacups. The handles on coffee cups appeared before handles were added to tea bowls, and coffee cups remained straight-sided, while the shallower body of teacups was always rounded or curved. Some potteries copied the Chinese octagonal form, matching the saucer to the shape, and decorated them both with Oriental-style flowers and leaves.

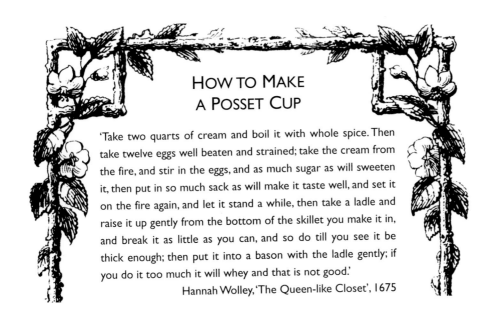

HOW TO MAKE
A POSSET CUP

'Take two quarts of cream and boil it with whole spice. Then
take twelve eggs well beaten and strained; take the cream from
the fire, and stir in the eggs, and as much sugar as will sweeten
it, then put in so much sack as will make it taste well, and set it
on the fire again, and let it stand a while, then take a ladle and
raise it up gently from the bottom of the skillet you make it in,
and break it as little as you can, and so do till you see it be
thick enough; then put it into a bason with the ladle gently; if
you do it too much it will whey and that is not good.'

Hannah Wolley, 'The Queen-like Closet', 1675

The manufacture of European and American porcelain teacups and saucers
dates back to the mid-eighteenth century when the secret of porcelain's recipe
was discovered and developed. At first, many manufacturers preferred to make
the smaller tea wares rather than large dinner plates, serving dishes and
tureens, for cups and saucers were less likely to warp in the kiln and the
factories therefore had to account for less wastage.

By the early nineteenth century, all the major English potteries – Spode,
Crown Derby, Chelsea, Minton, Royal Doulton, Wedgwood – were offering a
wide range of teacup designs and shapes. Crown Derby acquired increased
status when King George III granted its founder William Duesbury the right
to call himself Porcelain Manufacturer to His Majesty the King and His Royal
Highness the Prince of Wales. The company became Royal Crown Derby
when Queen Victoria fell in love with the beauty of the porcelains made there.
Minton started producing porcelain tea wares at the very end of the
eighteenth century and sample books of available designs were sent out to
retailers, who took orders from customers. In 1810, a Minton tea set included
a teapot and stand, a slop bowl, a box for sugar, a milk jug, twelve cups with a

A page from a Crown Derby Porcelain Company brochure, c. 1885. (*Royal Crown Derby Museum*)

An advertisement for Tower Tea featuring the blue-and-white porcelains that were so popular towards the end of the nineteenth century. (*Twinings*)

small ring handle, twelve saucers, twelve straight-sided coffee cups and two bread-and-butter plates.

Poorer families treasured whatever they inherited or could afford to buy and used them only on special occasions. Pieces of porcelain were handed down through the generations and so prized possessions were displayed on shelves and in cupboards and used on very special occasions. As Marie Trevelyan described in her book *Welsh Life*, 1894: 'Then there is the corner cupboard. Scarcely a house or cottage in Wales is without a corner cupboard. In it are kept the household treasures in the shape of teacups and saucers, and ornamental china of every description. It is not at all unusual to see in the corner cupboard china cups and saucers of the period when handles were unknown, and teapots that were

'"How is your cup?" is a non-U equivalent of "Have some more tea?" or the like. Possible negative non-U answers are "I'm doing nicely, thank you" and "(Quite) sufficient, thank you." There is a well-known non-U affirmative answer: I don't mind if I do (but this was U about a century ago).'
Alan S.C. Ross, *Noblesse Oblige*, ed. Nancy Mitford, 1956

'The Ghost' by Charles Churchill (1731–64), English poet, refers to
'Matrons who toss the cup, and see
The grounds of fate in grounds of tea.'

manufactured when tea was first used.' And if a tea party was to be held, visitors were sometimes required to bring an extra cup and saucer or two. In Mrs Gaskell's novel *Mary Barton*, published in 1848, the Barton family are preparing for high tea with eggs, ham and bread etc.: "'And thou just go to Alice Wilson . . . and tell her to come and take her tea with us. . . . If she comes she must bring a tea-cup and saucer, for we have but half-a-dozen, and here's six of us," said Mrs Barton.'

And how was the saucer used? Did people really drink their tea from the saucer? The Swede Per Kalm assured his readers in his 'Account of His Visit to England', 1748, that 'when the English women drank tea they never poured it out of the cup into the saucer to cool it, but drank it as hot as it came from the teapot'. The verb 'to saucer' one's tea certainly existed and there are prints, photographs and paintings of tea being slurped from the saucer rather than from the cup. It seems that the deeper saucer of the eighteenth and nineteenth centuries was used by some to cool the tea and the tea was then drunk from it. It has been suggested that, later, the saucer was used only for slops and the cup was once again preferred. It seems likely that the use of the saucer for the consumption of tea depended somewhat on class – in much the same way as the addition of milk before or after the tea also had and still has associations of breeding. Among the Victorian working-class people of Flora Thompson's *Lark Rise to Candleford* (1973) the saucer played its part and 'Father might shovel green peas into his mouth with his knife, Mother might drink her tea from her saucer . . . but who could eat peas with a two-pronged fork, or wait for tea to cool after the heat and flurry of cooking'. However, grand ladies from stately houses would have severely disapproved of such lack of manners.

With the new fashion for 'afternoon tea' in the early nineteenth century, the trade in tea wares burgeoned and wealthy families all over Britain acquired sets of porcelain cups and saucers. Books of household management and etiquette began to give instructions on how the equipment should be arranged and used. In 1893, Lady Colin Campbell wrote in *Etiquette of Good Society*: 'Tea equipage is placed on a table near to the lady of the house, who herself dispenses the tea . . . The cups and saucers are smaller than those in use at other meals, and are of a more dainty and refined character. . . . The other accompaniments are also on a smaller scale – the spoons, sugar basin and tongs, cream jug, are distinctly small.'

To suit the needs of those drinking tea and nibbling sandwiches at buffet tea parties, the 'cup plate' with a larger oval saucer developed at the beginning of the nineteenth century. The cup sat in its little round ring at one end, leaving the other part of the saucer–plate free for dainty food items. The design re-emerged in the early part of the twentieth century and was known as a 'bridge set', since it gave the card players an ideal resting place for refreshment during the game. And the set was useful in any situation where guests were not seated close to a small tea table, as this short quote from *The Manners of the Aristocracy by One of Themselves* (1881) points out: 'White tablecloths are not used, but those embroidered with crewels on coarse linen

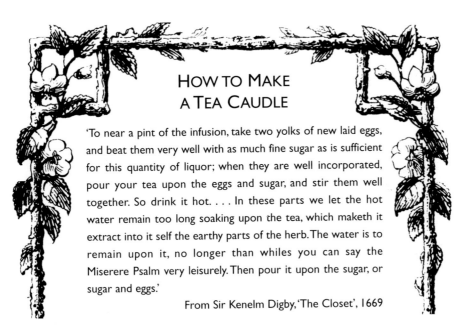

HOW TO MAKE A TEA CAUDLE

'To near a pint of the infusion, take two yolks of new laid eggs, and beat them very well with as much fine sugar as is sufficient for this quantity of liquor; when they are well incorporated, pour your tea upon the eggs and sugar, and stir them well together. So drink it hot. . . . In these parts we let the hot water remain too long soaking upon the tea, which maketh it extract into it self the earthy parts of the herb. The water is to remain upon it, no longer than whiles you can say the Miserere Psalm very leisurely. Then pour it upon the sugar, or sugar and eggs.'

From Sir Kenelm Digby, 'The Closet', 1669

Austrian cup and saucer in the style of Vienna, 1890–1900. The hand-painted, hand-gilded design is signed by the factory artist Ahne. (*John Pearman*)

or crash are fashionable. The saucers with a sort of fan-shaped projection for holding a piece of cake or bread-and-butter are most convenient, as they leave the hands more at liberty . . .'.

Everyone has his or her own idea as to what makes the perfect teacup. Some prefer wider tops, others prefer a narrow design. Some like pale colours, others like strong, dark decoration. The English novelist and poet May Sinclair created this charming conversation in her novel *A Cure of Souls* in 1924:

> The teacups – he noticed such things – were wide and shallow and had a pattern of light green and gold on white, with a broad green and gold band inside under the brim. His nostrils drank in the fragrance.
>
> 'I wonder why it is', he said, 'that a green lining to a cup makes tea so much more delicious. But it does.'
>
> 'I know it does,' she said with feeling.
>
> 'There's a house where they give you strong Indian tea in dark blue china. You can't imagine anything more horrible.'
>
> 'It would be.'
>
> 'And all teacups should be wide and shallow.'

'The outsider may indeed wonder at this seeming much ado about nothing. What a tempest in a tea-cup! he will say. But when we consider how small after all the cup of human enjoyment is, how soon overflowed with tears, how easily drained to the dregs in our quenchless thirst for infinity, we shall not blame ourselves for making so much of the tea-cup.'
Okakura Kakuzo, *The Book of Tea*, 1906

MY WISH.

I wish I were the china cup
From which you take your tea,
For every time you take a sip,
'Twould mean a kiss for me.

(*Twinings*)

The use of cup and saucer follows slightly different rules of etiquette for different situations. If a tea party is taking place around a dining table, it is quite correct to leave the saucer in its place on the table while the cup is lifted for drinking. However, if tea is served in the traditional way at low tables, then it is neater and more elegant to lift cup and saucer together before raising the cup to the lips. The saucer remains delicately balanced in the left hand while the cup is raised with the right. And whereas, historically, some thought it very refined to allow the little finger to trail outwards away from the other fingers, today such use of the hand might be seen as affectation. What is important is that a graceful cup and saucer of fine porcelain or bone china should be handled elegantly.

tea tables and trays

'We had Each our Own Little Table'

Until the end of the seventeenth century, few tables existed that were specifically designed for tea. They began to appear in the 1680s and by 1683 the Duchess of Lauderdale seems, as usual, to have been among the first to have acquired from the island of Java a tea table 'carv'd and gilt' upon which she served tea in her closet at Ham House. Since in its original form it was too low for English purposes, she arranged for the legs to be lengthened in order to bring it up to a more convenient height.

Lord Bristol also purchased a suitable table for tea and his *Expense Book 1690* records that he 'Paid to Medina ye Jew for a tea-table and two pairs of china cupps, £10'. And in 1693, according to household accounts, Margaret Bankes of Kingston Hall in Devon purchased a 'black Japan table for my closet'. Japanning or lacquering was extremely popular at the time and the Company of Patentees for Lacquering after the manner of Japan (founded in 1694) was offering for sale 'cabinets, secretaries, tables, stands, looking glasses, tea tables, and chimney pieces'. The Bankes family, probably typical of their

The eighteenth-century business card for William Russell showing samples of the tea tables and tea chests that he offered customers.

class, bought several more tea tables between 1700 and 1720 and household accounts record the following:

1702	a hand tea table £3. 0. 0
1705 July	a hand tea table of walnut tree 4/–
1709 March	a little hand tea-table 3/6
1711 Jan	a tea table and a pair of sconces £3. 10. 0
1717 July	a straw tea table 10/–

In fact, so many tea tables were by now being imported that London's cabinet-makers were worried about their own jobs. A petition by the Joiners'

Company at the end of the seventeenth century against the importation of goods from the East Indies states that '6,582 tea-tables had been imported within these four years'.

In households where there were none of the newly fashionable tea tables, salvers and trays were used instead. These were designed to sit atop another similar table that had edges to match the tray and little notches into which the feet of the tray fitted. In 1741, the 2nd Earl of Warrington acquired a pair of such tray/tables, which were described in the household inventory as '2 mahogany stands to set the silver tea and coffee tables on'.

Until the 1720s, quite plain square or rectangular trays were standard and from the 1720s, a circular form became more fashionable. During the eighteenth century the tray (or hand table as it was called) was recognised as an essential part of tea equipment and obviously needed to be wide enough to hold all the brewing utensils – including kettle, pot, canister, and the dishes and saucers used for drinking. They were often about 2 ft in diameter and, to make them easier to carry, hand-grips were added during the second half of the eighteenth century. The border was often raised into a pie-crust edge or fretted gallery to prevent bowls and dishes from slipping off. Some of these trays were designed to sit on a 'birdcage' that allowed it to be revolved for easier serving.

It was important that servants knew how to clean and look after tea trays and tables. Thomas Cosnett's *The Footman's Directory, and Butler's Remembrancer* of 1823 instructed:

In cleaning tea-trays you must not pour boiling water on them, particularly on paper or japanned ones, as it will make the varnish crack and peel off, and so spoil the look of them; therefore have a sponge wetted with hot water, and a little soap if the tray be very dirty, then rub it with a cloth; if it looks smeary, dust a little flour on, then rub it with a dry cloth. If the paper tray gets marked, so that you cannot get it off as before directed, take a piece of woollen cloth with a little sweet oil, and rub it over the marks; if anything will take it out, this will.

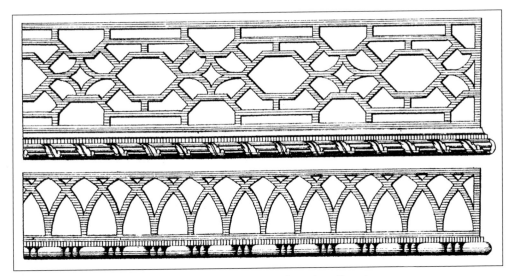

Eighteenth-century designs for fretwork to decorate the edge of tea trays.

Even after the increased availability and popularity of tea tables, salvers and trays continued to serve an important purpose and provided an easy way of delivering a welcome pot of tea to any part of the house at any time of day or evening. In December 1785, the actress Fanny Burney noted in her diary during a visit to Windsor Castle, quoted from *The Diary and Letters of Madame D'Arblay*, 3 vols, London, Vizitelly & Co., 1890:

In the evening while Mrs Delaney, Miss Port and I were working together in the drawing room, the door opened and the king entered. . . . And next Miss P goes out, walking backwards, for more candles, which she brings in two at a time, and places upon the tables and pianoforte. Next she goes out for tea, which she then carries to His Majesty upon a large salver, containing sugar, cream, and bread and butter and cake, while she hangs a napkin over her arm for his fingers.

As more and more specially designed tea tables were acquired, they inevitably became the focal point of social life in many households and a certain Mrs Pendarves wrote to Mrs Ann Greville in 1727 to complain that

'Our mornings, to tell the truth, are strangely dangled, and I, who am no friend of idleness, am obliged to saunter away a great deal of time . . . I am summoned to breakfast at my aunt's tea table, the ceremony of which generally lasts till twelve!' For many, the prattle and gossip that went on around the tea table was anything but attractive or appealing, as John Byng recorded in his diary in 1794, quoted in *The Torrington Diaries*, 1954: 'On my return I found Mrs Byng at tea, with some ladies of our house; and joining them, pass'd a dull hour in the much no-discourse of a tea-table.' However, almost a century later, in 1875, Dr Talmage of New York extolled the joys of sociable gatherings around the tea table in his *Around the Tea Table*: 'At breakfast we have no time to spare, for the duties of the day are clamouring for attention; at the noon-day dining hour some of the family are absent; but at six o'clock in the evening we all come to the tea-table for chit chat and the recital of adventures. We take our friends with us – the more friends, the merrier . . .'.

Between 1750 and 1775, tea tables were often referred to as 'silver' or 'china' tables after the tea wares displayed upon them. In North America, rectangular china and tea tables were made in great numbers and were widely used in thousands of homes. However, after the Boston Tea Party in 1773, ladies abandoned both their tea-drinking and their tea tables, provoking the anonymous composition of 'A Lady's Adieu to her Tea-Table':

> Farewell the Tea-board with your gaudy attire,
> Ye cups and ye saucers that I did admire;
> To my cream pot and tongs I now bid adieu
> That pleasure's all fled that I once found in you.
> Many a sweet moment by you I have sat,
> Hearing girls and old maids to tittle and chat
> And the spruce coxcomb laugh at nothing at all,
> Only some silly work that might happen to fall.
> No more shall my teapot so generous be

In filling the cups with this pernicious tea,
For I'll fill it with water and drink out the same,
Before I'll lose LIBERTY that dearest name,
Because I am taught (and believe it is fact)
That our ruin is aimed at in the late act,
Of imposing a duty on all foreign Teas,
Which detestable stuff we can quit when we please.
LIBERTY's the Goddess that I do adore,
And I'll maintain her right until my last hour,
Before she shall party I will die in the cause,
For I'll never be govern'd by tyranny's laws.

Designs for Pembroke tables with exquisite inlaid work and folding flaps to give flexibility of use.

In Britain, many different designs of tea table were created. Some were large enough to hold all the tea-making equipment and these took their place near the hostess so that she could attend to the brewing and serving. Others were smaller and were intended as a resting place for the individual cup and saucer of a particular guest – a feature mentioned by a certain Miss Hamilton when recording her visit to Mrs Delaney at Bulstrode: 'It was customary to have tea at seven, the groom of the chamber coming to say it was ready . . . We had each our own little table.' Some tables were fashioned in Chinese style with Oriental patterns executed in fretwork and applied work around the frieze. Some had a hinged tilt-top and a baluster base and could be stored against a wall and brought out at tea time. Some examples had tops that were divided into smaller compartments made to hold teacups and saucers or plates and dishes at supper time.

The famous Pembroke table, with its folding leaf, appeared in the mid-eighteenth century and was inspired by an elegant dining table of similar design. The Pembroke was intended for use in a lady's private drawing room and was for serving tea and for other light refreshments or small meals. In Jane Austen's unfinished novel, 'The Watsons' (probably begun in 1804), Tom Musgrave arrives as a surprise at the Watsons' home: 'As it happened, he did not give more surprise than he received when, instead of being shown into the usual little sitting-room, the door of the best parlour . . . was thrown open, and he beheld a circle of smart people whom he could not immediately recognise, arranged with all the honours of visiting round the fire, and Miss Watson seated at the best Pembroke table, with the best tea-things before her.'

All tea occasions needed a table of some kind or another and, as the years went by, the furniture requirements changed very little. For intimate gatherings, a smaller version of the tea table was adequate, as Marie Bayard advised in 1884 in *Hints on Etiquette* and continued with guidance on 'Daily Afternoon Tea': 'The time for tea is from four o'clock until half past five. A small gipsey table should be kept for the purpose of holding the tea-tray, or one of the wicker-work afternoon-tea tables, with shelves underneath for the

THE DUCHESS OF LAUDERDALE

Elizabeth Murray, Countess of Dysart and later by marriage the Duchess of Lauderdale, was a seventeenth-century leader of fashion, a lady with very expensive tastes and a knack of acquiring rich husbands. While still married to her first husband, Sir Lionel Tollemache, she became the mistress of the 2nd Earl of Lauderdale, whom she later married to become his duchess. She is also said to have been the mistress of Oliver Cromwell. Elizabeth was a very strong character and a leading figure at the court of Charles II and a friend of his wife, Catherine of Braganza. The Queen was a regular visitor to Ham House, the Duchess's home just outside London at Richmond, and the Duchess made quite sure that it was richly decorated and furnished in a style that was truly fit for a queen. The house was described as 'furnished like a great prince's' with tapestries, damask, velvet, mohair and other luxurious and costly fabrics. The Duchess was once described as 'a woman of great beauty, but of far greater parts; she had a wonderful quickness of apprehension and an amazing vivacity in conversation'. However, she had bad points as well: 'she was restless in her ambition, profuse in her expense.' She had elaborate new wrought-iron gates installed at the entrance to Ham House in order to impress the King and Queen when they came to visit and in her closet she had all the latest teas and equipment so as not to disappoint the tea-loving Catherine.

plates of cake and bread-and-butter.' Thomas Cosnett's *The Footman's Directory, and Butler's Remembrancer* told servants what sort of tray to use for different occasions:

If the lady makes tea in the drawing-room . . . have a tea-tray well dusted, and the cups and saucers put on, one for each, with a teaspoon to each; . . . let the teacups and saucers be put on the near side, so as to face the person who makes the tea, with the teapot, cream-jug, and slop-basin on the off side; and let the tea caddy be put near; if there be an urn-rug, do not forget it. If you have to wait at tea, that is, to hand it about to the company, you must have a small hand-waiter. Perhaps you may have to carry the tea and coffee up stairs to the company ready-made; if so you must be careful not to slop the tea over the cups into the saucers . . . Your tray ought to be pretty large, so you can put the bread and butter, sugar-basin, or any thing else upon it; take care to arrange them so that the ladies may take the cups with ease, and hold the tray low enough for that purpose.

In the USA, *Vogue's Book of Etiquette* recommended the same arrangements: 'When tea is served informally a low table is placed beside the hostess and a tea cloth spread over it. The tea things are brought in on a tray by the maid or a butler (or, in small houses where there is the minimum of service, by the hostess herself). On this tray are the hot water kettle, the teapot, cream pitcher, sugar bowl, cups and saucers, teaspoons, a small plate of lemon, sliced very thin, and sometimes a tea caddy or tea ball.'

Late Victorian rattan tea tables offering hostesses plenty of space for arranging tea cups and saucers, teapot, kettle, milk jug and sugar bowl for an afternoon tea party. (From Mrs Beeton, *Book of Household Management,* 1892)

Guidelines for arranging a tea tray in the first half of the twentieth century.

The ceremony continued through the years with all the same rituals. Editions of Mrs Beeton's *Book of Household Management* from 1892 to the 1930s recommended that 'Tea is served upon small tables, the servant before bringing it in seeing that one is placed conveniently near her mistress, who generally dispenses the tea.' In 1872, *Manners of Modern Society* highlighted the importance of the position of small tea tables at an afternoon tea: 'The furniture should be so arranged that the rooms may look full, and yet progress be not impeded. Tables and chairs should be so placed that the guests naturally form themselves into little groups, and can with ease pass from one knot to another.'

For larger, formal buffet teas a long table was covered with white cloths and servants stood behind dispensing the cups of tea. Mrs Heaton Armstrong explained this in her book *Good Form A Book of Everyday Etiquette*, 1889: 'The tea-table is generally wheeled into a bay-window or recess, so as to leave the room as free as possible, and the servants stand behind it and pour out.'

Servants were kept busy at such events carrying cups of tea around the room to the thirsty guests. *Manners of Modern Society* instructed: 'The servants should be expert and handy, as there is a good deal of waiting to be done. One should hand the cups of tea on a waiter, together with sugar and cream.' Mrs Heaton Armstrong well understood the organisational problems at tea-time events:

> Fashionable ladies find that pouring out the tea is an interruption to conversation, and that very often they have to be bidding farewell to one visitor when they ought to be mastering the great problem as to whether a second one takes sugar in his tea . . . The hostess finds that matters are greatly simplified by doing away with the tea-table in the drawing room, its place being taken by a neat-handed Phyllis, who bears a tray with a cup of tea ready poured out, and a cream-jug and sugar basin, and allows the visitor to settle the great sugar question for himself.

An early twentieth-century afternoon tea table set with all the necessary tea equipage placed near the hostess's place, a silver muffin dish and an elegant selection of tea-time foods.

Well into the twentieth century, servants were still much in demand at tea time, as recorded by Arnold Palmer in *Moveable Feasts*, 1952: 'tea was by now a formal affair, with cake stands, hot dishes and small trays borne to and fro by footmen who remained in attendance throughout the meal.'

New designs and clever tea-time inventions were welcomed into British homes. Typical of the period, the 7 November 1891 edition of *Beauty and Fashion* carried a small article on the latest furniture designs: 'Some of the most elegant afternoon tea-tables that could adorn a lady's drawing-room were beautifully made in blue and yellow majolica, designed after the style of Indian wood-carving.' In the 5 December issue there was a description of a 'Surprise Table', which it said 'was one of the most cute contrivances that we have ever seen. When spread open it held a tray upon which were deposited cups and saucers etc for afternoon tea. By closing over the wings of the table, the tea service vanished beneath, without leaving a trace of its identity; and this in a moment, tidiness prevails, and in the event of an unexpected visitor appearing upon the scene there is no necessity for the presence of a domestic to abolish all signs of the meal.'

In 1932, Mary Woodham comments on a most convenient new style of tea table in *Table and Domestic Etiquette*: 'A plan that is growing in favour, and which has much to recommend it, is for all the requisites to be set on a trolley, and for the trolley to be wheeled into the room to a convenient spot. The requisites for drinking go on the upper tier; and the cakes, bread and butter, on the lower. All jugs, cups and the teapot are stood with the handles to the right and spoons are placed in the saucers on the right of the cups.' Even Queen Mary liked the idea of the trolley, as Gabriel Tschumi revealed in *Royal Chef*, 1954: 'Afternoon Tea was served promptly at four-thirty every day at Marlborough House . . . By 4 pm everything needed for the meal would have been set out in readiness . . . Then as the clock struck the half-hour a footman wheeled it into Queen Mary's sitting-room on a trolley.'

'The fear of being thought pedants hath taken many young divines off from their severer studies, which they have exchanged for plays, in order to qualify them for the tea table.'
Jonathan Swift (1667–1745)

The Palm Court at the Waldorf Hotel, London, 1908. The room, designed specifically as a tea lounge, was at the heart of the hotel.

Tea-drinkers everywhere will recognise the tables, trolleys and trays described in the last few pages, for they have continued to be the focus of tea-drinking occasions over the centuries. We have all at some time lifted a small table into just the right position, gently pushed the trolley into place before the fire or out on to the terrace, or carefully carried the tray of tea things to a cosy corner and then gratefully relaxed into our place in the group to drink a refreshing cup of tea and talk quietly with our friends. The style and design of these familiar pieces of furniture may have changed over the years, but the purpose and the importance have stayed exactly the same.

jars, bottles and canisters

'A Pound of Tea with ye Bottle'

During the first 150 years of tea-drinking in Europe, the leaf was treated as a rare and expensive indulgence suited to the more elegant and refined parts of the home, kept within easy reach of those who were to drink it and brewed and served only by the master or mistress of the house. Its purchase was not casually left to the maid or housekeeper. Instead, it was personally bought from a specialist merchant by a high-ranking and trusted member of the household staff, if not by the householder himself. The details of quantities acquired were not entered in the household accounts along with rice, flour, sugar and other such everyday requirements, but were invoiced separately on the smart purchase orders of such reputable apothecaries and merchants as Thomas Garraway of Change Alley and R. Twining of Devereux Court, Strand.

The kitchen of a grand seventeenth-century house was no place for this costly luxury. And so,

'Tea! thou soft, thou sober, Sage, and venerable liquid, thou female tongue running, smile smoothing, heart opening, wink tipping cordial, to whose glorious insipidity I owe the happiest moments of my life, let me fall prostrate.'
Colley Cibber, *The Lady's Last Stake*, 1708

Chinese porcelain tea jar and matching tray, 1750. Jars like this would have been displayed on mantelshelves and tables in closets and withdrawing rooms along with other Oriental porcelains. (*National Trust Photographic Library/Andreas von Einsiedel*)

after purchase, the loose-leaf tea was carried home to be stored in fine red earthenware and porcelain jars, bottles and canisters that stood next to teapots and dishes in the closets of fine houses. These jars, like other porcelain table wares, came from China and Japan and were much admired for the skilful and colourful designs that decorated them. Originally designed by the Chinese to hold oil and subsequently adapted as tea containers, most were flat-sided or round and had neat little, tight-fitting, pull-off lids that acted as a measure so as carefully to transfer the loose leaf to the teapot. If the delicate top was sadly lost or broken, it was often replaced with a silver replica.

In 1682, Queen Mary of Holland paid 'for a pound of tea with ye bottle . . . 80 gilders 6 stivers', and this could have been fashioned in stoneware or white or clear glass. And in January 1702, according to household accounts, Margaret Bankes of Kingston Hall paid 'for a teapot 3/6, for a kenester 3/6', while, at Dyrham Park, William Blathwayt, according to an inventory of 1710, owned '5 Tea Potts, a Tea pott & Canister'. The word canister originally meant a box of tea weighing between 75 lb and one-hundredweight but by 1710 it was used to refer to small tea containers used at the table.

As with other tea wares imported from the East, European potters copied the shape and style of the foreign workers and created their own versions of the tea jar. Some potters replicated the typical Chinese flat-sided or round-bodied form, while others chose more fanciful shapes – fluted, octagonal, ovaloid or designs resembling fruits, vegetables and human figures. The domed cap on its elegantly narrow neck was gradually replaced by a shorter neck and sliding panel and this eventually became a flat or hinged cover.

Worcester tea set from 1770, with its bottle-shaped tea jar and generous slop basin. (*National Trust Photographic Library/Andreas von Einsiedel*)

Most European canisters were worked in stoneware, or, once the secret of its manufacture had been learned, in porcelain, although glass and enamel were also used. Following the Chinese tradition, several of the English potteries decorated their tea jars with enamelled designs of countryside scenes, flowers, birds and groups of human figures, and sets of these, often made to fit inside an enamel box or chest, were very popular among European buyers.

The different jars and bottles were often fitted with engraved silver caps bearing the words 'Green' and 'Bohea'. And those who could afford them had their jars made in silver, often in pairs and, again, inscribed with 'G' and 'B'. The inner compartment was usually made of lead, which was discovered to keep the tea fresh for a greater length of time, and in the base a sliding panel allowed the jar to be easily refilled. The fashion for engraving tea boxes continued through the centuries and a pair of containers made in 1723 by Edward Gibbons were decorated at a much later date with the words 'Mixed Tea' and 'English Breakfast Tea'.

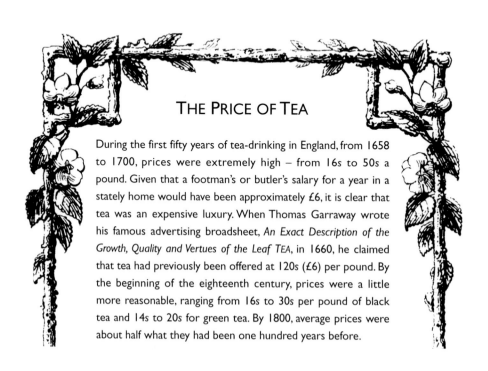

THE PRICE OF TEA

During the first fifty years of tea-drinking in England, from 1658 to 1700, prices were extremely high – from 16s to 50s a pound. Given that a footman's or butler's salary for a year in a stately home would have been approximately £6, it is clear that tea was an expensive luxury. When Thomas Garraway wrote his famous advertising broadsheet, *An Exact Description of the Growth, Quality and Vertues of the Leaf TEA*, in 1660, he claimed that tea had previously been offered at 120s (£6) per pound. By the beginning of the eighteenth century, prices were a little more reasonable, ranging from 16s to 30s per pound of black tea and 14s to 20s for green tea. By 1800, average prices were about half what they had been one hundred years before.

From the early eighteenth century, gold and silversmiths matched the skill of the potters and glass-cutters in the manufacture of globular, octagonal and flat-sided silver tea canisters. As the demand for these fashionable silver wares grew, so the shape began to change and many typical silver containers took on a squatter, rectangular form. Decoration became more elaborate and by the 1750s Rococo designs covered the round, oval, square and vase-shaped boxes with detailed landscapes, coats of arms, shells and fanciful swirls of plants and flowers.

'Bohea is the fav'rite through the whole town
The mode from the satin unto the stuff gown;
Both Tag-rag and Bob-tail will have their delight,
And strip themselves naked, but that they'll come by
If these be the pleasures of their lives,
Fate defend us from Tea-drinking Wives.'
'The Gossips Delight', c. 1760–90

Glass canisters followed the shape and size of porcelain and pottery jars and were given silver and gilt mounts and finials. An advertisement placed by Christopher Haedy in the *Bath Chronicle* on 20 November 1766 announced: 'To be sold by hand (in Bath). The stock in trade of a German who was the first that brought the art of Cutting and Engraving of Glass from Germany, Consisting of great variety of Cut, Engraved and Gilt glasses: fine Pyramids and Girandoles . . . Fine curious Glass Tea chests . . .'.

Goldsmiths now also offered matching sugar boxes to accompany the two tea canisters to the table. Since tea's introduction to Europe, sugar was almost universally added to the cup and at first was presented as small broken pieces on a shallow dish or plate. Now the wealthy added to their prestigious table equipage by ordering matching fine silver canisters in which to offer the sugar. *The Gentleman's Ledger 1735–1744* of London Goldsmith George Wickes notes that in 1735 a customer bought for £11 19*s* '3 Canisters for a Tea Chest'. In 1741 another client paid £18 17*s* 6*d* for a 'Sett of Cannisters & Sugar Dish and Graving 3 Coats to a Case'. At Dunham Massey in Cheshire, an inventory of the silver owned by the 2nd Earl of Warrington (who died in 1758) included 'gilt tea canisters' and, at Knole, the Duchess of Dorset also owned a gold tea canister.

On consul tables, mantelshelves, cupboards and sideboards in elegant withdrawing rooms and closets in grand houses around Europe, teapots,

Two silver tea caddies. On the left is a Chinese silver tea caddy made by Hung Chung, who made tea wares for Westerners in Canton in about 1880. It has an applied prunus decoration on a plain background. On the right is a nineteenth-century Dutch silver tea caddy made as a copy of a mid-eighteenth-century example. (*J. & S. Stodel*)

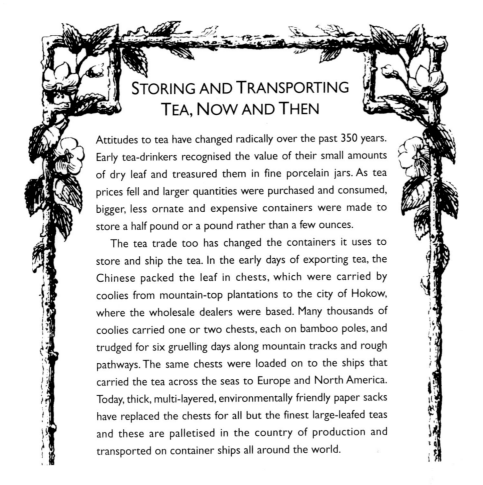

STORING AND TRANSPORTING TEA, NOW AND THEN

Attitudes to tea have changed radically over the past 350 years. Early tea-drinkers recognised the value of their small amounts of dry leaf and treasured them in fine porcelain jars. As tea prices fell and larger quantities were purchased and consumed, bigger, less ornate and expensive containers were made to store a half pound or a pound rather than a few ounces.

The tea trade too has changed the containers it uses to store and ship the tea. In the early days of exporting tea, the Chinese packed the leaf in chests, which were carried by coolies from mountain-top plantations to the city of Hokow, where the wholesale dealers were based. Many thousands of coolies carried one or two chests, each on bamboo poles, and trudged for six gruelling days along mountain tracks and rough pathways. The same chests were loaded on to the ships that carried the tea across the seas to Europe and North America. Today, thick, multi-layered, environmentally friendly paper sacks have replaced the chests for all but the finest large-leafed teas and these are palletised in the country of production and transported on container ships all around the world.

drinking bowls, vases, dishes, clocks and other decorative ornaments sat gracefully alongside fine tea jars, canisters, boxes and bottles – expensive containers fashioned to hold an expensive commodity. Perhaps the wealthy people of Europe had begun to understand the Oriental appreciation of the tea-drinking ritual and wished to surround themselves with all the beautiful objects associated with it. For, as Okakura Kakuzo so eloquently explained in *The Book of Tea*, 'Teaism is a cult founded on the adoration of the beautiful among the sordid facts of everyday existence. It inculcates purity and harmony, the mystery of mutual charity, the romanticism of the social order. It is essentially a worship of the Imperfect, as it is a tender attempt to accomplish something impossible in this impossible thing we know as life.'

'The Prevalence of Locks and Keys'

As the need and desire for fashionable and refined equipage grew among the tea-drinking rich, so the idea developed to lock away both the tea and the sugar in a beautifully crafted chest with a lock and key. The intention was to keep the tea safe from the pilfering fingers of the housemaids who by this time, like all members of the working class, had acquired a taste for tea. And as the key to the chest was closely guarded by the lady of the house or her housekeeper, there could be no chance of serving girls removing even the tiniest sample.

In 1729, Jonathan Swift wrote in *Directions to Servants* of 'small chests and trunks, with lock and key, wherein they keep the tea and sugar'. And Mrs Delaney wrote in 1740 of a 'very neat tea chest' that she had purchased for a friend 'which shall be filled with tea and delivered to her'. These chests were defined in 1775 as 'a small kind of cabinet in which tea is brought to table'. And just as before, when porcelain, glass, silver and enamel jars were proudly displayed in the elegant rooms where the tea was to be drunk, these chests and

Six Designs of Tea Chests

Published according to Act Parliament 1762.

Tea-chest designs by Chippendale from the eighteenth century.

boxes were also designed as fine ornamental household items that had a decorative as well as a practical purpose.

Jonathan Swift went on from describing these new containers to expressing his understanding of how they would inevitably spoil the servants' pleasures. In his *Directions to Servants by an Upper Servant*, published in the 1740s, he told 'The Waiting Woman':

> I pity you with all my heart!
> Your ladies play so mean a part,
> As now-a-day, old clothes to barter
> For china, trinkets, scented water,
> Or use them up for chairs and screens,
> Less'ning an honest servant's means;
> Besides yet shabbier plans than these,
> The prevalence of locks and keys!
> Making you live, all hugger mugger,
> On Bohea slops and coarse brown sugar.

And Daniel Defoe gave similar 'Advice to the Waiting Maid' in his *Directions to Servants* of 1745. He wrote of the 'execrable Custom got among Ladies . . . the Invention of small Chests and Trunks, with Lock and Key, wherein they keep Tea and Sugar, without which it is impossible for the Waiting-maid to live. For, by this means, you are forced to buy brown Sugar, and pour Water upon Leaves, when they have lost all their Spirit and Taste.' To make up for their own lack of leaf tea, household servants made sure that none of the dregs left over from their mistress's brew were wasted, as grand ladies often discovered. The following extract is from Duncan Campbell's 'A Poem upon Tea', 1735:

> My Suky Dainty and Bess Taste, the Cook,
> Will drink it sitting in the Chimney-nook,
> I often catch them draining what I leave . . .

The first casket-shaped wooden chests date from the reign of Queen Anne (1702–14) and had two or sometimes three lead-lined, lidded compartments for black and green tea and a separate section for sugar. The chests that protected the tea from potentially greedy, tea-slurping maids were crafted to hold either their own made-to-measure jars and canisters or the

Early nineteenth-century crystal tea caddy with ornate lock and trim. (*The Tea Council*)

porcelain, glass and silver jars and smaller boxes that were already in use. The *London Chronicle* for December 1766 refers to 'Several sets of silver mounted blue glass Tea canisters in Shagreen Chests'.

By this time, canisters were commonly made in sets of three to store two different types of tea and

A charming advertisement for Doctor's China Tea showing the lady of the house measuring tea carefully from a decorative metal caddy into the teapot, 1940s. (*Author's Collection*)

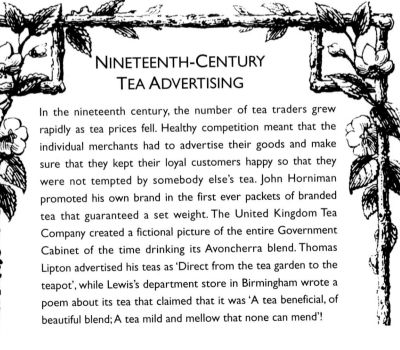

NINETEENTH-CENTURY TEA ADVERTISING

In the nineteenth century, the number of tea traders grew rapidly as tea prices fell. Healthy competition meant that the individual merchants had to advertise their goods and make sure that they kept their loyal customers happy so that they were not tempted by somebody else's tea. John Horniman promoted his own brand in the first ever packets of branded tea that guaranteed a set weight. The United Kingdom Tea Company created a fictional picture of the entire Government Cabinet of the time drinking its Avoncherra blend. Thomas Lipton advertised his teas as 'Direct from the tea garden to the teapot', while Lewis's department store in Birmingham wrote a poem about its tea that claimed that it was 'A tea beneficial, of beautiful blend; A tea mild and mellow that none can mend'!

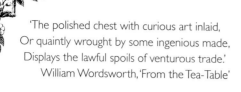

'The polished chest with curious art inlaid,
Or quaintly wrought by some ingenious made,
Displays the lawful spoils of venturous trade.'
William Wordsworth, 'From the Tea-Table'

sugar. People have often speculated that the third container or bowl was used for blending the tea, and this may indeed be true, but the evidence from cabinet-makers of the time was that it was in fact intended for sugar. This is verified in *The Cabinet-Makers' London Book of Prices* for 1793, which gives estimates for internal fittings of tea chests including a 'hole cut to receive the sugar bason' and 'making a case for the sugar bason to lift out'. During the reign of George I (1714–27) chests sometimes had two central compartments – one for lump sugar, one for powdered. Such 'Bite and Stir' boxes were also popular in North America, where it was quite common for a small lump of sugar to be placed in the mouth in Russian style and the tea sipped through it.

Tea chests had by now become such an important part of cabinet-makers' work that their business cards and shop signs often included images of such objects. Richard Holmes, cabinet-maker and glass-grinder, ran his enterprise at the sign of 'The Tea Chest' in Barbican in about 1783. And Joseph Cooper of Snow Hill, London, included on his trade card a list of wares, including 'Tea Chests of the most curious English and Foreign Woods', as recorded by Sir Ambrose Heal in *The London Furniture Makers*, 1953.

Wealthy customers were not difficult to find. On 24 November 1799, Sir Richard Colt Hoare bought for £2 20s from Thomas Chippendale 'a real Mahogany Tea chest with 2 wood canisters and 2 bottles with flush handle on top'. It is evident from inventories and household accounts at Stourhead that, by 1783, Sir Richard Hoare Bt. owned 'a neat Sattinwood Tea Chest banded with tulipwood, lind with skyblue velvet, silver double bolted lock + two neatly cut oval glass canisters, with oval silver covers and joints', for which he had paid '£7. 17. 6'.

Clients could choose to have extra details added to the tea chests that they commissioned. *The Cabinet-Makers' London Book of Prices* for 1793 contains the following specification for an oval tea chest:

A Oval Tea-Chest

Eight inches and a half long, five inches and a half wide, and five inches and a half high, veneer'd the long way, a string in the top and bottom corners, the bottom groov'd for cloth, the inside of the top and the rim of ditto veneer'd, a lining one inch and a half down in the bottom part, stands up to form a bead and steady the top, two canisters made to the sweep in three thicknesses, the top of the canisters flat and hing'd, and the inside of ditto lin'd with tin foil   1   4   0

Extras

Each inch, more or less, in length	0	0	10
If veneer'd cross-ways with curls	0	0	8
A cover with hole cut to receive a sugar-bason	0	0	6
Blocking ditto to the circle, and lining with cloth	0	0	5
Making a case for the sugar-bason to lift out, the inside shap'd to the circle, the outside to sit the sweep, top part veneer's and miter'd	0	1	6
If the bason is oval, the case to be extra	0	0	6
Half oval tops to the canisters, each	0	0	9
Banding – See Table of ditto			
Making cauls for the canisters to be paid for extra, if a single one, To be extra	0	2	0

Sometimes the base of a casket featured a secret drawer that slid open to reveal the key to the chest, a mote spoon, a set of teaspoons and a 'caddy' spoon. For, by now,

A nineteenth-century mahogany tea chest. Inside are three interior compartments for sugar and tea. (*The Tea Council*)

the boxes and jars that fitted inside these elaborate chests were known as 'caddies', a word derived from the Malay *kati* – a measure of approximately 1⅓ lb. And, in time, these objects themselves became known as caddies as well as chests. In his *Cabinet Dictionary* of 1803 Sheraton explained that 'The word "caddy" is now applied to various kinds of tea chests, of square, octagon and circular shapes.' The word was used both for large chests with two or three compartments and for single-chamber containers crafted to resemble pears, apples, pineapples and melons, as well as sarcophagus shapes and oval, square or rectangular boxes. These smaller, lockable, single-compartment boxes were particularly fashionable between 1762 and 1789.

The importance of the appearance of these prestigious tea containers led cabinet-makers and goldsmiths to choose expensive, rare and highly decorative materials for their work. Tortoiseshell, mother-of-pearl, rare woods, silver and crystal were all used and often enhanced with marquetry, fine carving, japanning, penwork, engraving, paper filigree work and the addition of fancy mounts, hinges and handles. In 1791, Princess Elizabeth was given by Charles Elliott 'fifteen ounces of different filigree papers, on ounce of gold paper' with a 'box made for filigree work with ebony mountings, lock and key, and also a tea caddy to correspond with the box'. In 1786, the *New Lady* told its readers that the art of filigree curled paper work 'affords an amusement to the female mind capable of the most pleasing and extensive variety, it may be readily acquired and pursued at very trifling expense'. The curling, rolling and gluing of coloured strips of paper created what the magazine called 'A profusion of neat elegant patterns and models of ingenuity and delicacy suitable for tea-caddies . . .'.

The key to the caddy was, of course, crucial. For, without it, no tea could be brewed and the assembly had to go thirsty. William Cowper in a letter to his friend Lady Hesketh in 1793 reminded her that she had taken her caddy key with her when she had gone away, leaving him as her house guest but without access to a supply of the leaf. In a letter to a friend, E. Williams of Aberystwyth wrote, as recorded in *From the Morganwg Letters*, National Library of Wales:

My dear Friend –

I am carried to the Abbey by two gentlemen from Germany who are travelling in search of information. . . . They will take tea here and I suppose politeness will make it proper that I should tarry with them . . . at all events I shall return as early as possible and enclose the key to my Tea Caddy . . . and beg thee to direct my servant to provide Thee with Tea apparatus when I trust thou will feel thyself perfectly at home as I always wish thee to feel under my humble roof.

In North America, after the Boston Tea Party of 16 December 1773, tea was abandoned as a favoured beverage, and in the port of Greenwich, then the largest town in the state of New Jersey, 'citizens of the quiet Jersey village hurried to their doors on that night, December 22, 1773, as shrill war whoops sounded and a lurid glow lit the low-lying clouds. The hated tea, together with the chests that contained it, was burned in the middle of the Market Square . . .' (from William Ukers, *All About Tea*, 1935). It is not clear if the chests mentioned were the large wooden chests that carried the tea from China to Britain and onward to the shores of North America, or the small ornate caskets used in the domestic setting. No matter. The symbolism of the burning remains the same – tea had been given up for the sake of liberty. But

the sacrifice was not total and did not endure for long. George Washington gave regular tea parties, and, some time in the following century, tea-lover Ralph Waldo Emerson re-established the American love of the rejected drink when he wrote in *Letters and Social Aims*, published in 1876: 'There is a great deal of poetry and fine sentiment in a chest of tea.'

Storage caddy made for C. Trau, tea merchants in Vienna, 1880. (*Demmer*)

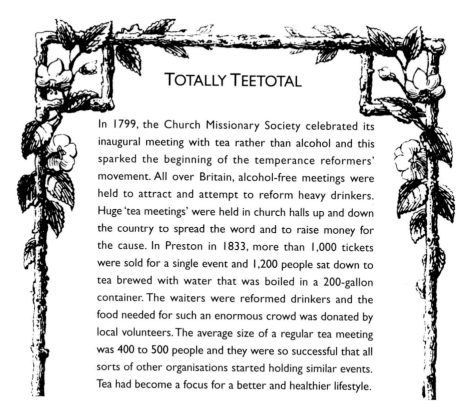

TOTALLY TEETOTAL

In 1799, the Church Missionary Society celebrated its inaugural meeting with tea rather than alcohol and this sparked the beginning of the temperance reformers' movement. All over Britain, alcohol-free meetings were held to attract and attempt to reform heavy drinkers. Huge 'tea meetings' were held in church halls up and down the country to spread the word and to raise money for the cause. In Preston in 1833, more than 1,000 tickets were sold for a single event and 1,200 people sat down to tea brewed with water that was boiled in a 200-gallon container. The waiters were reformed drinkers and the food needed for such an enormous crowd was donated by local volunteers. The average size of a regular tea meeting was 400 to 500 people and they were so successful that all sorts of other organisations started holding similar events. Tea had become a focus for a better and healthier lifestyle.

An almost inevitable development of the tea chest and caddy was the teapoy. This piece of furniture appeared at the very end of the eighteenth century and was a free-standing chest on one or more legs designed to contain teas, sugar and various silver spoons. The word derives not from 'tea' but from the Hindi word *tin* meaning 'three' and the Persian word *pae* meaning 'foot' – for most teapoys were indeed three-footed. In his *Collaction* [*sic*] *of Designs for Household Furniture and Interior Decoration 1808*, George Smith illustrated two teapoys and referred to them as 'used in Drawing Rooms etc. to prevent the company rising from their seats when taking refreshment . . . these articles may be manufactured in mahogany, rose-wood, or bronzed and gilt, to suit the different rooms they may be placed in'. And Simmons in his 1850 *Dictionary of Trade* described the teapoy as 'an ornamental pedestal table with lifting top, for holding tea'. The majority of teapoys were made between 1820 and 1850 and usually contained four compartments for different teas and two for sugar bowls.

The ritual surrounding the tea caddy was prominent through the nineteenth century, when tea continued to be an expensive beverage associated with elegant living and upper-class etiquette. Even after the price had gradually dropped, making tea so much more accessible to the middle and working classes, much prized and valuable tea wares still held an important place in the everyday ceremonies of upper-class households. Gabriel Tschumi, in his book *Royal Chef*, 1954, describes tea time in the royal household, where he worked during the reign of George V:

> Queen Mary made the tea herself, carrying out all the steps necessary with precision and care. They included measuring the Indian tea she liked best from the Jade Chinese tea-caddy kept in the cabinet in her sitting room. . . . If Queen Mary was fatigued she sometimes delegated the duty of tea making to a lady-in-waiting. This involved a further small ritual, for the cabinet contained many of Queen Mary's treasures, and was always kept locked . . . At times an incautious hand with the tea-caddy would draw from the Queen the reproof: 'Level spoonful. Don't waste it, now.'

However, as tea became cheaper and cheaper towards the end of the nineteenth century, extravagant and elaborate caddies were used less and less. Supplies of tea found their way to the kitchen instead of the drawing room and the valuable chests that had once guarded the leaf became purely decorative objects – as they still are today in many homes. Cheaper tin boxes were manufactured and decorated with the branded names and logos of the tea companies selling them. The advertising design and company name was either hand-painted on to the metal or applied in the form of a printed paper label that was pasted on. The style used was influenced over the years by the works of famous artists of the time – Charles Rennie Mackintosh, Toulouse Lautrec, William Morris, etc. – but also reflected tea's links with the East. So Indian elephants, Japanese geishas, Eastern temples and Chinese landscapes all found their way on to these colourful tins.

12
caddy spoons

'Measure for Measure'

The expensive Chinese porcelain jars used by the first European tea-lovers had their own little measure in the form of a small, tightly fitting lid. The leaves could be shaken carefully out of the jar into the cap and then tipped into the teapot. But the shape and style changed over the years and the tall jar gradually became somewhat squatter, lost its narrow neck and cap and acquired instead a hinged lid or sliding cover. So, with the lid altered, some sort of measuring spoon became essential. The earliest examples of these date from the 1760s and were in fact long-handled ladles – an adaptation perhaps of an ordinary household flatware spoon with a slightly shorter handle than normal. Some Georgian and Regency chests have a special recess for a ladle with a 5- or 6-in handle.

A shell-shaped, nineteenth-century, solid-silver caddy spoon, the design influenced by the real scallop shell that Chinese tea merchants included in their export tea chests in the seventeenth and early eighteenth centuries.

Gradually the handle was shortened in order to fit the spoon neatly inside the tea chest so that it was always there when needed. The first short-handled caddy spoons appeared in England in the 1770s, in Holland in the 1780s and in Russia in the 1820s and introduced the more fanciful and decorative shapes that so many collectors seek today. One of the earliest most popular shapes was the

Leaf-design caddy spoon, Birmingham, 1817.

scallop shell, the idea taken from the real shells that the Chinese tea merchants are said to have thoughtfully placed inside the tea chests that were shipped to Europe and North America. The shell provided a perfect scoop for brokers and merchants in the European docks as they examined the teas before buying. Goldsmiths and silversmiths, therefore, saw their chance to offer the tea-loving public a charming and useful design to add to their tea wares. And so 'cadee shells' found their way into many homes in Europe and North America.

Caddy spoons were as much a part of the tea equipage in North America as in Britain, and, in 1792, the set of tea silver made by Paul Revere for John Templeman of Boston included a shell-shaped caddy spoon as well as a caddy, a strainer and a set of sugar tongs. In the 1800s, to rival the shell, caddy spoons in the form of leaves, jockey caps, thistles, acorns, shovels, eagle wings, hands, fish and Chinese mandarins appeared.

Hand-shaped caddy spoon, London, 1805.

So the measuring of tea into the pot was easy, as Thomas Babington Macaulay (1800–59) explained:

> Pour varlet, pour the water,
> The water steaming hot!
> A spoonful for each man of us,
> Another for the pot!

When Mrs Beeton's *Book of Household Management* was first published in 1861, although she made no mention of the relatively new custom of taking 'afternoon tea', she did discuss the plant and the basic rules for brewing a good pot: 'There is very little art in making good tea; if the water is boiling, and there is no sparing of the fragrant leaf, the beverage will almost invariably be good. The old-fashioned plan of allowing a teaspoonful to each person, and one over, is still practised.' It is clear from Charles Oliver's *Dinner at Buckingham Palace*, written in the early 1900s, that when tea time came around in the royal

Collection of silver caddy spoons from a Bonhams auction catalogue, 28 January 2000. (*Bonhams*)

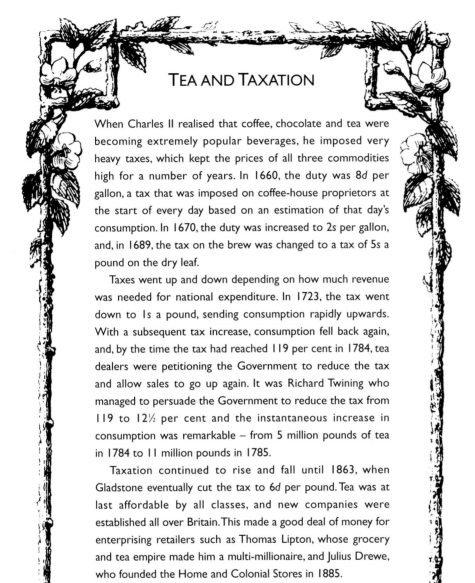

TEA AND TAXATION

When Charles II realised that coffee, chocolate and tea were becoming extremely popular beverages, he imposed very heavy taxes, which kept the prices of all three commodities high for a number of years. In 1660, the duty was 8*d* per gallon, a tax that was imposed on coffee-house proprietors at the start of every day based on an estimation of that day's consumption. In 1670, the duty was increased to 2s per gallon, and, in 1689, the tax on the brew was changed to a tax of 5s a pound on the dry leaf.

Taxes went up and down depending on how much revenue was needed for national expenditure. In 1723, the tax went down to 1s a pound, sending consumption rapidly upwards. With a subsequent tax increase, consumption fell back again, and, by the time the tax had reached 119 per cent in 1784, tea dealers were petitioning the Government to reduce the tax and allow sales to go up again. It was Richard Twining who managed to persuade the Government to reduce the tax from 119 to 12½ per cent and the instantaneous increase in consumption was remarkable – from 5 million pounds of tea in 1784 to 11 million pounds in 1785.

Taxation continued to rise and fall until 1863, when Gladstone eventually cut the tax to 6*d* per pound. Tea was at last affordable by all classes, and new companies were established all over Britain. This made a good deal of money for enterprising retailers such as Thomas Lipton, whose grocery and tea empire made him a multi-millionaire, and Julius Drewe, who founded the Home and Colonial Stores in 1885.

household in Queen Mary's time it was the Queen herself who took charge of the measuring spoon: 'The ritual of the English tea-time was brought to perfection by the late Queen Mary, for whom it was the favourite time of day . . . Queen Mary would take over and meticulously measure out her favourite Indian tea from a jade tea-caddy she kept locked in a cupboard . . .'.

As tea's price dropped, it was viewed as a more ordinary, everyday commodity and was stored in the kitchen instead of in the drawing room. And just as the containers in which the tea was kept became less opulent and showy, so the caddy spoon was less frequently made from silver or silver plate. It became available in chrome and other cheaper metals, often as souvenirs from holiday resorts or as useful advertising gifts or special offers from individual tea companies.

Caddy spoon, Birmingham, 1807.

The caddy spoon continued to play an important part in the tea-brewing ritual throughout Europe and North America until tea bags started to replace loose tea in many kitchens. As the popularity of tea bags increased and the use of loose-leaf tea declined, the golden rules for perfect brewing were similarly lost or forgotten. Those who wisely persist in choosing loose tea over tea bags have found it more and more difficult to buy the correct measuring spoons, which should contain approximately $2\frac{1}{2}$ g of leaf. A teaspoon obviously holds much less and is a poor substitute. Modern caddy spoons are available, often in the familiar shell design, but are not easy to find. For those who wish to own a little piece of history, antique dealers, markets and auction houses offer fine old caddy spoons, but at a high price.

Caddy spoon, 1760.

teaspoons and sugar tongs

'A Piece of Sugar the Size of a Hazelnut'

From the very earliest years of tea-drinking in Europe, sugar was added to the brew. Herbal drinks were widely mixed with sugar to ease the natural bitterness, and, as tea was advertised and sold as a herbal tonic, sugar was almost automatically added to the cup. In 1675, Philippe Dufour wrote: 'add a dram of tea to a pint of boiling water, let it stand for about seven minutes, then pour it into earthenware or porcelain cups into which a piece of sugar, or sugar candy, the size of a hazelnut had been placed. Alternately, the sugar could be held in the mouth and the tea supped as hot as possible through it.' In Russia, of course, this latter method of sweetening tea was popular and Alexander Pushkin wrote, 'Ecstasy is a glass full of tea and a piece of sugar in the mouth.'

Since tea in those early years was served in wealthy surroundings for aristocratic, elegant people, beautiful silver spoons for stirring sugar into tea also became a crucial part of the refined tea equipage. An inventory of the Earl of Dorsett's plate made on 'July 6th 1697 att London, Knowl, & Copthill'

Sugar tongs and tea spoons from a Bonhams auction catalogue. From centre, clockwise: cast sugar tongs formed as twigs with acorns, 1830; pair of early eighteenth-century tongs; spring-action tongs, 1775; various spoons from the eighteenth century; spring-action tongs, 1775; andiron tongs with shell grips, 1720; tongs with plain oval grips, 1730. (*Bonhams*)

lists '6 guilt Tea-spoons, 1 coffee pot, 1 chocolate pot & cover'. Households owned various small silver or gilded spoons, which no doubt served for other purposes as well as stirring sugar into tea. *Mercurius Politicus*, the London newspaper, mentioned various silver spoons in seventeenth-century lists of stolen property. These include 'wrought' spoons in 1685, 'small gilt' spoons in 1686, spoons 'with plain handles' and 'with twisted handles' in 1689, 'with knobs' in 1697, 'a long tea spoon' in 1697 and 'silver spoons with knobs made by T. Smith, Cheapside' in 1659. Similarly, in 1685, the *London Gazette* reported the theft of 'six little wrought silver tea spoons one tea pot'. The following year, the paper mentions 'three small gilt tea spoons'.

'Love and scandal are the best sweeteners of tea.'
Henry Fielding, *Love in Several Masques* (1728)

Since the porcelain bowls from which tea was gently sipped held only a dainty couple of mouthfuls, the spoons to be used with them also had to be small. Although also intended for use with coffee and chocolate, the spoons quickly became known as teaspoons. They remained small until the late eighteenth century, when they almost doubled in size, but they reduced again from about 1870.

Saucers were also much smaller than today and so the fashion for sugar and the need for spoons provoked the introduction of special dishes on which to lay the spoons and sugar nippers when not in use. The oval silver trays were at first rather plain but in time were given a fancy fluted, scalloped or saw-toothed edge and four little feet on which to stand. After about 1760, these were no longer made and, as teacups and saucers grew in size, the spoon was subsequently placed in the saucer.

David Garrick's comedy *Bon Ton*, 1775, highlights the presence of silver sugar spoons on tea tables in London's pleasure gardens.

> Bone Tone's the space, 'twixt Saturday and Monday,
> And riding in a one-horse chair on Sunday.
> 'Tis drinking tea on summer afternoons
> At Bagnigge Wells with China and gilt spoons.

According to the will of Celia Fiennes, dated 1738, her possessions included six gilt teaspoons as well as a Japan tea chest, a silver kettle and canisters. In 1729, Charles Gardner paid a bill for the engraving of teaspoons and a sugar dish.

There were those who disapproved of the use of sugar in tea. In his treatise *The Abuse of Hot Liquors 1706* Dr Duncan of the Faculty of Montpelier wrote: 'Coffee, Chocolate and Tea were at first us'd only as Medicines while they continued unpleasant, but since they were made delicious with Sugar, they are become poison.' Others, as this extract from a Bedfordshire newspaper in 1784 reveals, discussed the advantages of adding sugar: 'It is now almost the universal practice in this kingdom to drink tea twice a day, as a part of our diet. Therefore, it deserves our attention to render the constant use of it as wholesome as possible, by

Silver sugar bowl, tea caddy, caddy spoon and sugar spoon from an anonymous pattern book of pieces by Matthew Boulton, c. 1785. (*Courtesy of the Trustees of the V&A*)

Detail from Richard Collins's painting *English Family at Tea*, showing covered silver sugar bowl, silver trivet made specially to hold the tea spoons and silver andiron sugar tongs, eighteenth century. (*Courtesy of the Trustees of the V&A*)

adopting the different qualities to our constitution – the black teas, bohea, congou, and souchong, are of an astringent nature, and are rendered more binding when sweetened with double-refined loaf-sugar. The green teas, singlo and hyson, are laxative, and are more opening when sweetened with fine Barbadoes clayed sugar, commonly called fine Lisbon sugar.' The addition of sugar to tea appears to have been widespread in Britain in the eighteenth century. François de la Rochefoucauld, a Frenchman who travelled widely in Britain, noted in *A Frenchman in England* in 1784 that 'The high cost of sugar or molasses, of which large quantities are required, does not prevent this custom being a universal one, to which there are no exceptions.'

Sugar was imported to Europe in the form of solid cones weighing about 6 lb, and these had to be broken into small pieces with cast-iron tongs and little choppers, and then, to make powdered sugar, crushed in a pestle and mortar. The smaller pieces of sugar or the granules were then served to the table in little porcelain dishes with nippers or a spoon. The very early nippers

109

DRESSED FOR TEA

By the 1880s, afternoon tea and tea parties were a very important part of social life throughout Britain. It was an essentially feminine time of the day when ladies gathered in each other's homes to gossip, exchange news and show off their latest hats and frocks. This was also the time of the 18-in waist, an unnatural phenomenon achievable only by the most uncomfortable and severe tight-lacing. The Dress Reform Society and sensible influential members of society pressurised the fashion industry to change the shape of women's clothing so that ladies could breathe more easily and retain the normal position of their internal organs. As a result of this, the tea gown was created.

Designed for comfort as well as elegance and indulgence, the tea gown evolved as a flowing, deliciously luxurious garment that looked marvellous whether or not whale-bone corsets were worn underneath. It was a dress for home and garden, not for tea in a tea room or hotel lounge, for the trailing skirts and flowing soft fabrics would not withstand dirty streets or indeed be suitable for 'visiting'. As Mrs Eric Pritchard told readers of *The Cult of Chiffon*, 1902: 'We cannot trail about the London streets in the flowing garments of beauty, but in our drawing rooms, when the tea urn sings at 5 o'clock, we can don these garments of poetical beauty.' Or, she suggested, 'It can also be donned with real effect between the hours of tea and dinner when a few friends drop in on a hot afternoon during the London season. The gown for the latter occasion should be a frou-frouing mass of lace and muslin, making the wearer look as fair and as cool as the conditions of London permit.'

of the late seventeenth century resembled miniature fire andirons. Between 1720 and 1730 these were formed to resemble little pairs of scissors, although by 1770 these had been gradually phased out and bow-shaped, sprung tongs made from one piece of metal had become more fashionable.

Early sets of tea-brewing and serving equipment often included spoons and sugar nippers. A set from 1735 comprised one-dozen teaspoons, a strainer, sugar nippers, two knives, three canisters and a cream jug. An inventory of Lady Audley's plate sent to London in 1797 included 'one silver tea urn, one coffee ditto, 2 pr tea tongs, 20 tea spoons, 1 tea pot, 1 tea caddy'. And in North America, where tea was as popular among groups of expatriate Europeans as it was in Europe, goldsmiths started offering sets of spoons as part of the essential tea equipage. In 1759, Joseph Richardson of Philadelphia ordered from his London suppliers '6 dozen of silver teaspoons with tongs and strainer to each half dozen in Shagreen cases'. In the same period in Britain, Sir Richard Hoare ordered various items of silver table wares for his home at Stourhead. His household accounts show that he purchased the following items from Makepeace & Harker, Serle Street, Lincoln's Inn Fields, Goldsmiths and Jewellers:

1812 May 26th
A pair of sugar tongs 1. 3. 0. . . .

May 7 A silver Tea pot after antique model 14. 10
Silver sugar bason

The drinking of tea involved certain rules of etiquette and if those at a tea gathering did not understand the subtlety of the rules, they could find themselves in very awkward situations. In 1782, the French Prince de Broglie was invited to take tea in a British home and afterwards recorded exactly what happened: 'I partook of most excellent tea and I should be even now still drinking it, I believe, if the Ambassador had not charitably notified, at the twelfth cup that I must put my spoon across it when I wished to finish with this sort of warm water. He said to me: it is almost as ill-bred to refuse a cup of tea when it is offered to you, as it would be indiscreet for the mistress of the house to propose a fresh one, when the ceremony of the spoon has notified her that we no longer wish to partake of it.' In 1823, Thomas Cosnett advised servants that 'You will easily know when they have done, by putting the spoon in the tea-cup.' But members of the household staff needed to know the other ways by which guests might indicate that they had drunk enough. In some houses, it was sufficient to tap the cup lightly with the spoon. The gentle tinkling alerted a maid or one of the gentlemen present to the fact that the cup should be removed. Or the empty cup could be turned upside down on its saucer, again signalling that no more tea was required.

In Scotland, it seems that teaspoons were numbered in order that the hostess, when gathering cups near her ready to pour second and subsequent cups of the brew, might ensure that each cup was returned, full, to its rightful owner. This was recorded by Alexander Boswell of Auchinleck in 1810 in his *Edinburgh or the Ancient Royalty, A Sketch of Former Manners*:

> Then were the days of comfort and of glee!
> When met, to drink a social cup of tea:
> The chequer'd chairs, in seemly circle placed;
> The Indian tray with Indian China graced;

A Cruickshank cartoon highlighting what could happen if the rules of tea-table etiquette were not understood. (*Twinings*)

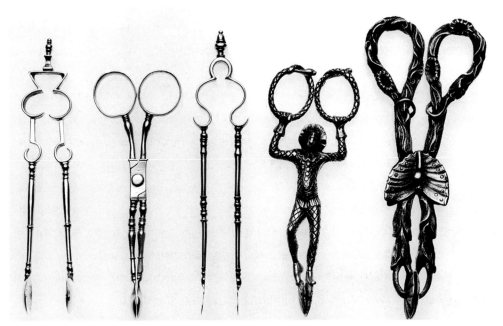

A collection of sugar tongs. From left to right: Dutch tongs with spiral twist arms and ring end, 1758; continental tongs, 1700; andiron-type tongs with oval grips and rat tails, 1726; sprung, engraved tongs with stylised leaf motifs, 1798; sugar nips with box hinge and shell grips, 1730. (*Bonhams*)

> The red stone Tea-pot with its silver spout;
> The Tea Spoons numbered,* and the tea fill'd out! . . .

And so sugar continued to be added to tea and many people today still prefer their tea sweetened. In *Lark Rise to Candleford* Flora Thompson describes how a newcomer to the hamlet found the tea difficult to drink without sugar: 'Christopher Holdenby only gradually grew accustomed to cottage fare. The tea was so strong that it set his teeth on edge, and the only way he could drink it was after it had been sweetened with four lumps or 2 dessert spoonfuls of

---

* 'the spoons all numbered' . . . 'This precaution of numbering the spoons enabled the attentive hostess to return to each guest the cup that had already kiss'd the lip, a gratification to squeamish fancies which cannot be hoped for now-a-days, when the slop is conducted behind the curtain.'

sugar.' The 6 April 1878 edition of the *Caterer and Refreshment Contractors' Gazette* criticised the British habit of over-sweetening tea:

> How to Make a Cup of Good Tea
>
> One great mistake made by the tea-drinker is that of sweetening tea too freely. In hotels and coffee-rooms, the customers, when permitted, play sad havoc with the saccharine supplies, and it has often been found necessary to limit the quantity supplied to each. The sugar is used, not to sweeten the tea, but to reduce its bitterness.

Today's use of sugar varies from country to country and must depend on personal choice. But advice from connoisseurs is to try each individual tea on its own before adding sugar or milk. Many teas have a soft sweetness and perfume of their own that is drowned by the flavour of sugar or honey. If, however, the tea is too strong, too pungent, too astringent or even slightly bitter, a little sugar can make it more palatable.

The following delightful extract from the company archives of J. Lyons indicates the importance of sugar in tea in our everyday lives. It is the jottings of the poor secretary or office girl responsible for brewing the tea to be served at board meetings.

> Board Meeting Service
>
> | | |
> |---|---|
> | Mr Brown | Tea no sugar |
> | Mr Lyons | Milk and Hot Water, no sugar |
> | Mr Monti Gluckstein | Tea and no Sugar |
> | Mr Isadore Gluckstein | Cocoa and no Sugar |
> | Mr Alfred | Tea, 2 Sugars (if wearing spectacles, weak, if without them, medium, if looking through them, strong, if looking above them, leave the room as soon as possible) |
> | Mr Marks | Milk and hot water, no sugar |
> | Mr Oatley | Tea and 1 sugar |
> | Mr Booth | Tea and 1 sugar |

14

milk jugs and creamers

'They Call them Milk Bottles'

There is no evidence that when tea was first drunk by Europeans milk was added. In mid-seventeenth-century paintings scenes involving tea-drinking, little dishes of sugar, teaspoons and sugar nippers are shown clearly as part of the equipage, but there are no milk jugs on the table. In France, Madame de Sévigné referred to 'le thé de cinq heures' and told a friend in a letter that she drank hers with milk. She also recommended it to her daughter in 1684 with both milk and sugar, which suggests that it was not the norm to add milk to one's tea.

It is possible that our use or not of milk in tea depended largely on any contact that may have taken place during the seventeenth century between

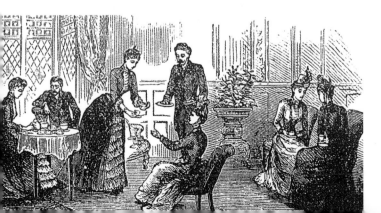

A Victorian hostess hands one of her afternoon-tea guests a cup of tea and offers the addition of a little milk.

Three-piece silver tea set with its elegant milk jug, late nineteenth century. Profusely decorated with embossed dragons and bamboo, the set was made in China for Europeans living there. Many tea sets like this were made for the 'foreigners' of Hong Kong, Shanghai and Canton and, although Chinese silver is rare in some forms, it seems that all Westerners acquired an Oriental tea set while there. (J. & S. Stodel)

Europeans and Chinese traders. The Chinese Manchus of the Qing Dynasty (1644–1800) drank their black China tea with milk and early Europeans who traded with them may simply have copied the habit. The Dutch drank what they called Melkthee, which may have originated as a result of an encounter between the Chinese emperor and a group of Dutch merchants in 1655. The Dutchman Jean Nieuhoff described the feast given for the Dutch delegation by the emperor that year: 'At the beginning of the dinner, there were served several bottles of The or tea, served to the table, whereof they drank to the Embassadors, bidding them welcome: This drink is made of the Herb The or Cha in fair water, which afterwards they boil until a third part be consumed, to which they adde warm milk about a forth part, with a little salt, and then drink it as hot as they can well endure.' In 1660, Thomas Garraway, in his advertising broadsheet entitled *An Exact Description of the Growth, Quality and Vertues of the Leaf TEA*, wrote that tea 'prepared with Milk and Water strengtheneth the inward parts, and prevents Consumption, and powerfully asswageth the pains of the Bowels, or griping of the guts and looseness'.

However, most Chinese drank (and still drink) green tea, rather than black, without milk. Their preference was perhaps transferred back to Europe by merchants and tea dealers who had met and traded with them rather than with members of the Manchu court.

As the seventeenth century progressed, a fashion for adding milk to tea developed in England. When Margaret, Lady Russell, came across some little milk bottles while shopping one day in 1698, she was so delighted with them that she wrote to her daughter, Lady Roos at Hadden, to say, 'Yesterday, I met with little bottles to pour milk out for tea; they call them milk bottles. I was much delighted with them, and so put them up to a present for you.' By 1702, vessels for milk were commonly known as 'milk potts' and the London Assay Office entered silver jugs as 'milk ewers' and charged one penny per pot for the assay. And in 1706 in Scotland, Lady Grisell Baillie's mother paid '1s 4d for a pot for milk to tea' to an Edinburgh shopkeeper. In the same year, the East India Company first included porcelain milk jugs and pots in their cargo. For those who preferred silver on their tea tables, the earliest silver milk and cream jugs were tiny and narrow, and stood only about 2½ to 3½ in tall. They had plain D-shaped handles, sharp little spouts rather like beaks, neat rim feet and often a domed lid – for the fashion at this time was for hot milk in tea.

As they became more necessary as a part of the tea equipment, and as silver tea wares generally became more popular, silver jugs were occasionally included in boxes that contained sugar nippers, strainer spoons, teaspoons, two tea knives, canisters and a sugar box. The Duke of Grafton had a set made for him by Richard Watts in 1712 that included a teapot, sugar bowl and milk jug with an ivory handle, a sharp spout and a high domed lid.

By the 1730s, small jugs for milk and cream were fairly common, although George Wickes, a London goldsmith, sold only two 'milk boats' and six 'cream ewers' in ten years to his customers. The shape had gradually changed from tall and narrow to pear-shaped, then helmet-shaped and eventually boat-shaped. The lid disappeared as the idea of hot milk in tea was abandoned by the beginning of George II's reign in 1727. When Robert Southey described a

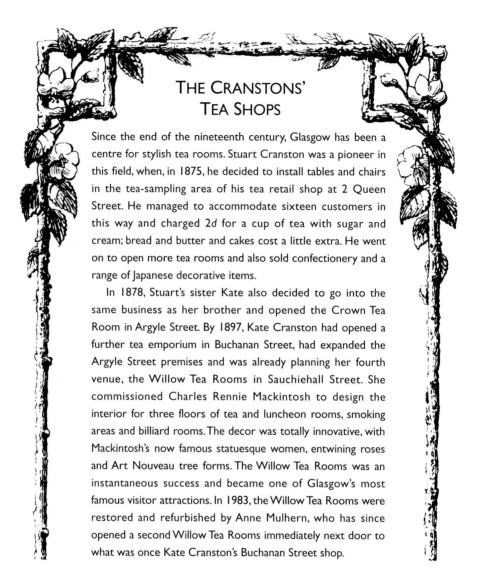

THE CRANSTONS' TEA SHOPS

Since the end of the nineteenth century, Glasgow has been a centre for stylish tea rooms. Stuart Cranston was a pioneer in this field, when, in 1875, he decided to install tables and chairs in the tea-sampling area of his tea retail shop at 2 Queen Street. He managed to accommodate sixteen customers in this way and charged 2d for a cup of tea with sugar and cream; bread and butter and cakes cost a little extra. He went on to open more tea rooms and also sold confectionery and a range of Japanese decorative items.

In 1878, Stuart's sister Kate also decided to go into the same business as her brother and opened the Crown Tea Room in Argyle Street. By 1897, Kate Cranston had opened a further tea emporium in Buchanan Street, had expanded the Argyle Street premises and was already planning her fourth venue, the Willow Tea Rooms in Sauchiehall Street. She commissioned Charles Rennie Mackintosh to design the interior for three floors of tea and luncheon rooms, smoking areas and billiard rooms. The decor was totally innovative, with Mackintosh's now famous statuesque women, entwining roses and Art Nouveau tree forms. The Willow Tea Rooms was an instantaneous success and became one of Glasgow's most famous visitor attractions. In 1983, the Willow Tea Rooms were restored and refurbished by Anne Mulhern, who has since opened a second Willow Tea Rooms immediately next door to what was once Kate Cranston's Buchanan Street shop.

British breakfast table in 1807, he wrote: 'The breakfast table is a cheerful sight . . . The tea is made in a vessel of silver, or of fine black porcelain; they do not use boiled milk with it, but cream instead in its fresh state, which renders it a very delightful beverage.'

There are countless references in literature and diaries from the period to make it clear that from the turn of the eighteenth century both milk and cream were added to dishes and cups of tea in Britain. In 1735, Duncan Campbell declared in 'A Poem upon Tea':

> Now all Philosophers agree,
> That Women shou'd drink MILK and TEA;
> It suits their constitutions best,
> And pleases th'unpolluted taste . . .

Jonathan Swift recorded the typical morning of a fashionable young woman in *Journal of a Modern Lady*, 1740:

> Now, loit'ring o'er her tea and cream,
> She enters on her usual theme;
> Her last night's ill success repeats
> Call Lady Spade a hundred cheats . . .

Foreign visitors to a country are always quick to notice everyday habits and, in 1748, Per Kalm noted in *Per Kalm's Account of his Visit to England*, 'most people pour a little cream or sweet milk into the teacup when they are about to drink the tea'. And an anonymous poem from Dublin demonstrates that the Irish enjoyed the same luxury in 1752:

> The leading Fair the Word harmonious gives;
> Betty around attends with bending knee.
> Each white-arm Fair, the painted cup receives;
> Pours the rich cream, or stirs the sweetened Tea.

Milk in tea was important to people at all levels of society. Most people bought their supply from the dairymaid who knocked on their doors and Boswell noted in his *London Diary* that during the reign of George III (1760–1820) arrangements were made specially for the milk for the King's tea to be delivered each day.

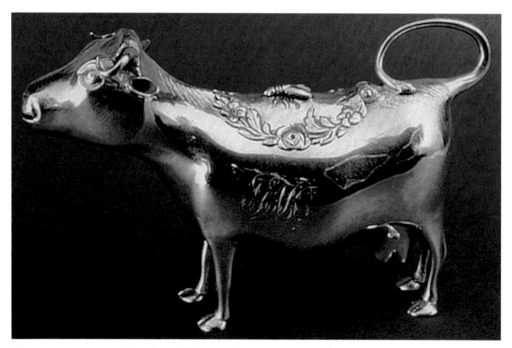

Silver cow creamer, a charming addition to the tea table in Georgian times and now often reproduced in white porcelain.

By the 1760s, creamers and milk jugs took on a barrel form, which had a slender neck and dispensed the liquid over a small, gently curling lip. Then, in the 1770s, one of the most charming and appealing items on the tea table was introduced – the cow creamer. Jugs in the shape of friendly cows were first made in Holland by John Schüppe and his design was eagerly imported to Britain. These attractive jugs were made in sections with the sides of the head and body, the legs and hooves, the horns, ears and tail handle all made separately then soldered together, and a hinged saddle fitted last as a lid, often with a bee or a fly forming the knob.

Although many European tea-drinkers chose to take their tea without milk (and most still do), the British palate developed a preference for a stronger brew to which milk and sugar have continued to be an important addition. Throughout the nineteenth century, the growing number of tea sets in porcelain, stoneware and silver always included jugs for milk and cream. Mrs Gaskell's novel *Cranford*, published in 1853, describes a typical Victorian afternoon tea scene: 'In a few

'As for my part, for Tea I've this to say,
If I ha'nt eat or drank for half a day,
A dish of Tea, with cream and butter'd toast,
Which does not cost above a groat, at most,
Pleases me full as well as boil'd or roast.'
J.B. Writing Master (pseudonym), 'In Praise of Tea –
A Poem, Dedicated to the Ladies of Great Britain', 1736

minutes tea was brought. Very delicate was the china, very old the plate, very thin the bread and butter, and very small the lumps of sugar. . . . In the little silver jug was cream, in the larger one was milk.' When William Ukers wrote *All About Tea* in 1935, he included his observations on the use of milk and cream in Britain: 'Milk or cream generally is added to the beverage in the cup. Cold milk is used by most people, but some prefer hot. It is placed in the cup before the tea is poured. In Scotland, where the cream is thin, it is used as a superior alternative to milk. In Western England, cream is not used much in tea as the milk is quite rich.'

Today, most tea-drinkers would not dream of adding cream or warm milk to their cup. The modern choice is limited more simply to cold skimmed, semi-skimmed or full-fat milk. But still people debate the age-old question as to whether it is correct to add the milk to the tea or the tea to the milk. It is hard to know what past etiquette dictated, but it would seem from comments and illustrations that, in 'polite society', the milk was added to the tea and

Black basalt cream jug, cup and saucer decorated with encaustic enamels and featuring a border design known as 'Running Anthemiom', c. 1775. (*Image by Courtesy of the Wedgwood Museum Trust Limited, Barlaston, England*)

A British family taking tea on the lawn, early twentieth century. (*Courtesy of the Trustees of the V&A*)

then stirred in with pretty silver teaspoons. Today, the scientific recommendation is to add the tea to the milk in order to achieve a better natural mixing. And scientific research has shown that, if full-fat or half-fat milk is added to boiling hot tea, there is a slight possibility of little globules of fat separating out on the top of the tea and leaving a greasy film on the surface. It is said that this can also change the taste of the tea. But, as with other questions of food and drink, there can be no black-and-white rules. Each person must decide which method is best and follow his or her preference. However, whatever type of milk is selected and at whatever stage it is added to the cup, the serving and drinking of tea still demand a vessel to contain the milk, and modern tea sets always include a small jug exactly for this reason.

15

mote spoons

'With Narrow Pointed Ends'

Antique mote spoons are among the prettiest and most charming of all silver tea wares. They appeared in the late seventeenth century to fulfil several purposes but sadly ceased to be a necessary part of the tea equipage in the late 1790s. A reference in the *London Gazette* in 1697 to these fragile, pointy handled spoons with their delicate perforations in the bowl described them as 'long or strainer teaspoons with narrow pointed ends'. But how could these shallow, dainty spoons possibly have acted as strainers? Those pouring tea would have had to execute their task incredibly slowly if the stream of golden liquor was not immediately to splash directly out again. It is far more likely that the spoons were used as an early type of measuring spoon that allowed any dust to fall away from the loose leaf while it was being carefully transferred from tea jar to teapot.

The mote spoon's second practical role was to scoop from the surface of the tea in the cup any unwanted and unsightly floating tea leaves that had escaped through the teapot spout – hence the development of the name 'mote spoon' or 'mote skimmer'. A third usage is thought to have been the necessary unblocking of the teapot spout when the swollen infused leaves hindered the stream of tea into the cups. It has been suggested that the sharp spike that

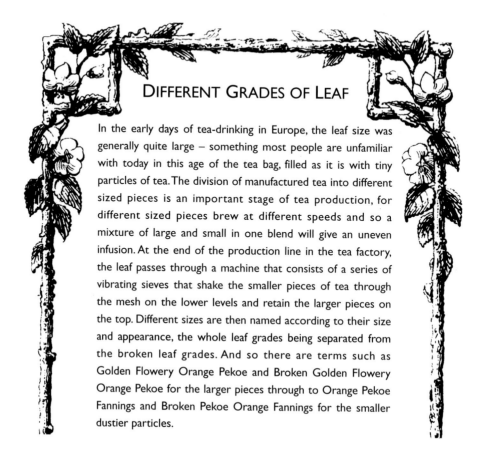

DIFFERENT GRADES OF LEAF

In the early days of tea-drinking in Europe, the leaf size was generally quite large – something most people are unfamiliar with today in this age of the tea bag, filled as it is with tiny particles of tea. The division of manufactured tea into different sized pieces is an important stage of tea production, for different sized pieces brew at different speeds and so a mixture of large and small in one blend will give an uneven infusion. At the end of the production line in the tea factory, the leaf passes through a machine that consists of a series of vibrating sieves that shake the smaller pieces of tea through the mesh on the lower levels and retain the larger pieces on the top. Different sizes are then named according to their size and appearance, the whole leaf grades being separated from the broken leaf grades. And so there are terms such as Golden Flowery Orange Pekoe and Broken Golden Flowery Orange Pekoe for the larger pieces through to Orange Pekoe Fannings and Broken Pekoe Orange Fannings for the smaller dustier particles.

Georgian mote skimmer and caddy spoon with Edwardian teaspoon and sugar tongs. (*Author's Collection*)

Fine, solid-silver mote spoon with its elegant arrangement of punched holes in the bowl and its typical long, pointed handle. (J. & S. Stodel)

formed the very tip of the handle was intended for piercing olives or mulberries from a punch bowl, but there is no evidence for this. The fact that mote spoons were included in boxed sets of silver teaspoons, or had their own special little groove inside the 'secret' drawers of tea chests, would seem to indicate that these exquisite items were indeed used at tea time. Although the prodding of spouts may not have been the most elegant part of the ceremony, it was no doubt essential.

The perforations in the earliest mote skimmers were simple, round, crudely pierced holes and the long handle that was soldered to the bowl was merely a thin wire of silver with a barbed end. But from the 1740s and 1750s, the bowls were punctured with more intricate and fanciful designs of scrolls, crosses, fretted parrots, leaf shapes and fleurs-de-lis.

As the tea strainer came into use at the end of the eighteenth century, the need for the mote spoon died away and those that remain are expensive but very beautiful collectors' items reminding us of earlier fashions in tea-drinking rituals.

tea strainers and infusers

'Restraining the Leaves'

Tea strainers first appeared in the 1790s and gradually replaced mote skimmers. Mote spoons and skimmers had been used to lift out any stray floating leaves from a cup of tea. It is unlikely that the 'strainer' bought by Joseph Richardson of Philadelphia in 1759 was a strainer that we would recognise today; it was probably a silver mote spoon – still in common use at that time. Strainers were designed to ensure that no leaves escaped into the cup in the first place. Teapots were sometimes given a built-in strainer at the base of the spout and this certainly helped when larger leaf teas were brewed. But smaller particles could easily find their way out and strainers were used to catch them.

Sir Walter Scott's reference to a strainer in *St Ronan's Well*, published in 1823, highlights a quirky misuse of tea in the early years of its consumption in Britain. It is said that a lady who had been sent a pound of tea by a friend as a gift knew very little about what to do with her expensive supply of the new Oriental herb and so boiled it up, served the liquor in cups and then offered the infused leaves to be eaten: 'A silver strainer, in which in times more economical than our own, the lady of the house placed the tea leaves after the very last drop had been exhausted that they might hospitably be divided amongst the company to be eaten with bread and butter.'

Tea-Leaf Superstitions

Tea has played such a central part in British social life for so long that all sorts of quirky superstitions have grown up around the teapot and the leaves. In some northern parts of England, it was said that a new housewife would not enjoy good luck until she had a teapot of her own and had brewed tea in it in the new home. In the West Country, it was seen as a bad omen to pour the boiling water into the pot when the leaves had been forgotten. If the teapot lid was ever left off in the south of England, a stranger would definitely arrive at your door. One lady pouring from another lady's teapot left herself open to some danger, as the saying went that she would become pregnant with twins who would certainly have ginger hair!

The leaves themselves played a major part in predicting good and bad fortune. In the fishing town of Hull, the teapot was never emptied out on the day before the man of the house set sail on a fishing trip. To swill out the infused leaves would have been interpreted as emptying him out of the house. And on board the fishing trawler, once the first pot of tea had been brewed and a second pot was needed, the used leaves were allowed to remain in the pot and more tea was added. It was hoped that, by heaping the tea into the pot, plenty of fish would be heaped into the hold of the boat. In Somerset, accidentally spilling tea leaves brought good luck, while, in the West Country, stirring the leaves inside the pot would always result in an argument or quarrel.

In 1923, Della Thompson Lutes of New York wrote in her book *The Gracious Hostess*: 'Tea may be made with a tea-ball, a tea strainer or in a pot. With the strainer, this article, made of silver, is filled (not too full) with tea, placed over the empty cup and the hot water poured slowly over it.' These instructions were highly misleading and show a misunderstanding of how tea should be brewed.

Danish tea strainer and tea bell designed by Johan Rohde for the firm of Georg Jenson. These two items were made to match others made in the 'Acorn' pattern, first produced by the company in 1915. (J. & S. Stodel)

The leaves need to move around in a generous quantity of boiling water in order to be able to release their flavour and colour. If trapped in a shallow strainer sitting on top of a cup this is certainly not possible. Also, the water should remain as hot as possible during the infusing time, preferably inside a lidded teapot. The water at the top of a cup cools quickly and would therefore hinder successful brewing in this situation. Strainers were not intended for this lazy way of making tea. Their specific and only possible role was, and still is, to be placed on the cup before the tea is poured from the pot through it into the cup.

As with so many elegant and charming pieces of tea equipment, strainers fell into disuse with the growth of the tea-bag market in the 1950s and 1960s and, like caddy spoons and sugar tongs, they have become merely collectors' items or museum pieces. It is such a shame, for it is with the assembled use of beautiful porcelains, silver wares and linens that tea time becomes something more than

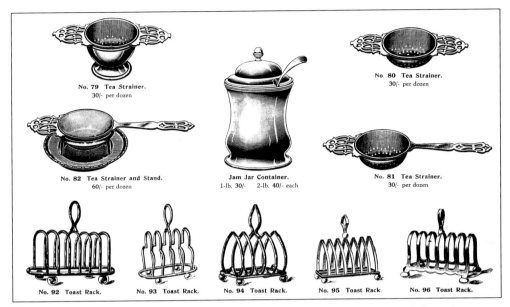

An illustration from the catalogue of Butler's of Sheffield showing their range of silver-plate tea strainers, 1916. (*Courtesy of the Trustees of the V&A*)

just a quick, practical 'tea break'. In Japan the tea schools have perpetuated the understanding of the tea ceremony and its place in society, its ability to calm and soothe and bring a sense of peace that the modern world obstructs. In Britain, we have forgotten how to prepare tea 'properly' – how to brew it and how to serve it – and a tea bag dangled for a few seconds in a mug neither provides a flavourful cup of tea to revive the body nor creates an ambience to refresh the spirit. Treat tea with respect and care, brew it properly, serve it

Brass strainer with generous supports for safe positioning on wider cups, 1950s.
(*Author's Collection*)

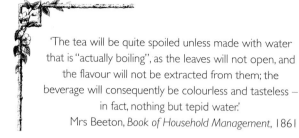

'The tea will be quite spoiled unless made with water that is "actually boiling", as the leaves will not open, and the flavour will not be extracted from them; the beverage will consequently be colourless and tasteless – in fact, nothing but tepid water.'

Mrs Beeton, *Book of Household Management*, 1861

elegantly and it will reward you a hundredfold.

Whenever strainers are still used, it is vital to make sure that each tea served has its own strainer. If only one strainer is provided for several different teas, the risk is that leaves from one tea already in the strainer will taint a different tea as it is poured through that same strainer. This is particularly important in tea rooms and hotel tea lounges, where staff sometimes fail to meet this crucial standard of tea service. Etiquette also demands that the strainer is lifted very carefully from cup and replaced on the strainer rest or drip catcher before then being placed over the next cup or back on to the table. The drip catcher must be close to the strainer in order to prevent unsightly brown drip stains appearing on crisp white linen tablecloths.

In order to brew perfect tea, it is advisable to separate the infused leaves from the infusion at the end of the recommended steeping time. With this in mind, tea-ware designers have over the centuries made many attempts to create brewing equipment that facilitates that separation. Infusers have appeared many times as an integral part of teapots and as reusable baskets and balls that can be placed inside almost any brewing vessel. As long ago as 1873, Mrs Beeton's *Book of Household Management* informed readers about the latest infuser available at that time:

The Tea-Float is a very useful addition to the tea-pot. The tea is placed in the float, and the float in the tea-pot. Boiling water is added as in ordinary tea-making. The float rises to the surface and thus retains the tea at the hottest part of the water, instead of sinking to the bottom, which is the coldest part. By this application of natural laws and the chemistry of tea-making, all the strength of the tea is withdrawn, and the infusion is far stronger than when prepared in the usual way. A smaller quantity of tea is therefore required when the tea float is used. The float can be procured of all grocers, tea-dealers etc. and is from 1s to 1s 6d in price.

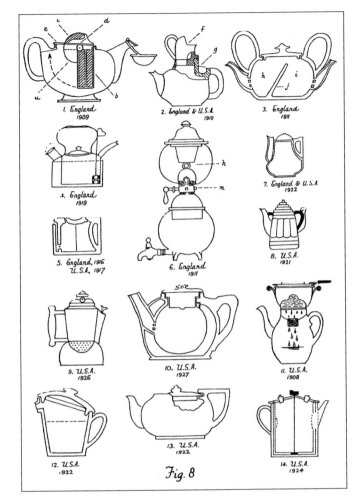

1. England 1909
2. England & U.S.A. 1910
3. England 1911
4. England 1919
5. England, 1916 U.S.A, 1917
6. England 1911
7. England & U.S.A. 1922
8. U.S.A. 1921
9. U.S.A. 1926
10. U.S.A. 1927
11. U.S.A. 1908
12. U.S.A. 1922
13. U.S.A. 1922
14. U.S.A. 1924

Fig. 8

A variety of inventive teapots and tea kettles from the early twentieth century. (From William Ukers, *All About Tea*, 1935)

The science of water temperatures and the suggestion that tea brews best at the top of the teapot are questionable, but the idea of the infuser float was a good one, for it allows the removal of the leaves before the tea becomes stewed and bitter. The ideal infuser or 'float' must be big enough to allow the leaves to absorb water and then move around while they swell and release their wonderful qualities and flavours.

In 1895, Mappin & Webb promoted a Unicas patent tea infuser 'to make a cup of tea without using a teapot'. This was a teaspoon with a wire mesh covering the bowl of the spoon, which when made in electroplate cost 3s 6d

The "Universal" Tea Ball Tea Pot

Every woman knows Tea leaves should not steep too long, that Tea Balls are drippy and inconvenient. In the "Universal" the Tea Ball remains in the Pot, and when the

An American advertisement from *The Ladies' Home Journal*, 1911.

and in silver cost 11*s* 6*d*. The 15 June 1896 edition of *Caterer & Hotel-keeper's Gazette* described the 'Teaette':

. . . tea-infuser patented by Mr George Gray of 114 Great Russell Street, London, WC. It consists of a deep bowl spoon, perforated with small holes and slits, and having attached to it by hinges and duplicate spoon-bowls. A screw attached to the handle near the bowls serves to keep the top one in position. The idea is that the spoon should be filled with the requisite quality of tea and then plunged into a cup or pot full of boiling water, and withdrawn after a few minutes infusion. The 'Teaette' should be most useful for travelling luncheon baskets, and might be introduced by caterers in tea-rooms, offering lady customers their own caddy's 'teaettes' and jug of boiling water. The novelty of the idea might catch on.

Given the early invention of such brewing spoons and other infusing devices, it is perhaps surprising that it took until about 1910 in the USA for someone to think of making a tea bag out of silk and then paper! Della Thompson Lutes had a much clearer understanding of how to use infusers than she showed regarding the role of strainers (see page 127). She wrote in *The Gracious Hostess* that, if tea is 'made in a tea ball, the water is poured, boiling hot, from the kettle to the cup. The filled tea ball is immersed and allowed to remain until the hot water is sufficiently flavoured.' Since those days, infusers have been made from muslin, nylon, metal, plastic, stoneware, porcelain and paper and the search for the perfect design continues.

17

tea sets

'A Pretty Little Tea Set upon a Small Table'

Once Oriental porcelains had reached the shelves and counters of shops and stalls in London and beyond, those that could afford them purchased little bowls for their tea, elegant jars in which to store the leaf, tiny little red earthenware teapots and dishes on which to offer bread and butter and pieces of lump sugar. But it was rare for these various items to match each other and the only similarity was often coincidental due to the fact that blue decoration on a white ground was the most common form of Oriental design. Europe's 'Chinamen', the porcelain traders, had to try and make sets up themselves as best they could.

At first, the English East India Company did not itself include porcelains and earthenwares on its list of goods to be imported and instead the individual officers were granted the right to bring such goods into Britain and sell them for their own profit. Whatever space their goods took up was not counted as part of their allocated space on board and the only stipulation was that the boxes containing their booty must not exceed 13 in in height. These were stashed in

'There are few hours in life more agreeable than the hour dedicated to the ceremony known as afternoon tea.'
Henry James, *The Portrait of a Lady*, 1881

the lowest parts of the ships to form a solid base on which the tea chests were stacked.

Gradually, the East India Company realised the potential of the porcelain trade and asked their agents to organise cargoes of bowls and pots as well as tea. However, it was not always an easy operation and the costs paid to the agents in China, Japan and India were high. In 1685, the company sent a letter to an agent in China to say, 'We can now but briefly tell you that we are amazed at the prices you have invoiced to us, your own goods from Chyna, being 50 per cent as near as we can guess more than they will bring here . . . the thea cups [are] dear at 1d a piece.' And in 1686, more complaints were voiced because 'we have since exposed ye China ware to sale which yielded but £1,053 . . . and when ye buyers had paid for several lots upon view of them found them crack'd and refused to take them away so that their money was to be returned to them'.

Most collections of tea bowls, dishes and saucers in Europe's grand houses were an odd assortment of whatever could be found. However, gradually a system was developed whereby sets of matching porcelains could be ordered from Chinese and Japanese factories and these could be decorated with a specific design, family coat of arms or motto. Orders were lodged with the captains of the individual East Indiamen ships, or with an agent in the relevant country, and the entire process, from placing the order to receiving the goods in Europe, could take as long as two years. As with cups, teapots and tea canisters, the European potteries copied the goods arriving from China and often imitated not just the form but also the designs used for decoration. On 13 April 1757, the *Public Advertiser* wrote: 'We hear that this day and tomorrow will finish the sale at the new auction-room in Spring Garden of the Bow China, and that there will be exhibited large table services of the finest old Japan patterns.'

As Gladys Scott Thomson explained in *Life in a Noble Household*, 1940, each member of an aristocratic family during the early years of the eighteenth century would have acquired a set of tea-drinking equipment:

TEA IN ASSAM AND DARJEELING

Until the 1830s, all the tea consumed in Britain came from China. The only other tea-producing country at the time was Japan, but the herbal green teas grown there were not to the taste of the British palate. But as consumption went up, more and more British silver was being paid to the Chinese merchants. There was really nothing the Chinese wanted from Britain as a balance of trade, except opium, which was being grown by the British on their territory in India and imported illegally into China via a devious network of middle-men.

As a result of the amount of money being paid to China for tea and because of increasing problems involved in dealing with China, the British had been for some time investigating other land on which they could establish plantations of their own. In 1788, the botanist Joseph Banks was asked to prepare a report on the possibility of tea production in India. He wrote that it was possible and that the climate was favourable, but nothing further was done to progress the idea.

In 1823, a Major Robert Bruce informed the East India Company that tea grew wild in Assam, and eventually in 1834 a committee was set up to oversee the acquisition of tea seeds from China and the cultivation of new plants for commercial production in north-eastern India. It took a further four years of experimenting with different seeds and plants and the input of experienced Chinese growers before the first tea had been plucked, processed and shipped to London for auction, where it was declared very satisfactory. Once plantations had been successfully established in Assam, tea production expanded up into Darjeeling, which is still today one of the world's most important tea-growing areas.

. . . every purchase of tea was, just as had been the coffee, at first earmarked for some particular individual and the resemblance was continued in that each member of the family acquired his or her own little tea-set. . . . The china sets that came to Woburn along with the tea were very much more expensive than those provided for the rival beverage. Lady Margaret Russell received a set of tea dishes – bought for her by her father's steward for £1.14 0d and three years later another set of 6 for twenty shillings and a tea salver (tray) for five shillings.

As tea became more and more popular in houses such as Woburn, more tea equipage was acquired and so cupboards and display cabinets were filled with beautiful silver and porcelains from the best manufacturers in China and Europe.

At the beginning of the eighteenth century, a set of equipment needed for brewing and serving tea included a small round or pear-shaped teapot, a lidded milk jug, a covered sugar bowl, a pair of scissor-shaped sugar tongs, a basin for slops, a dish for teaspoons, a kettle and burner and a lockable tea caddy. Some of these items would have been made of silver, others of porcelain, and the lockable caddy would have been made of shagreen, rare wood, ivory, tortoiseshell,

A bone-china Wedgwood tea set, 1815. The pieces are decorated with landscapes painted by John Cutts. Each view is named on the base or reverse of the item. (*Image by Courtesy of the Wedgwood Museum Trust Limited, Barlaston, England*)

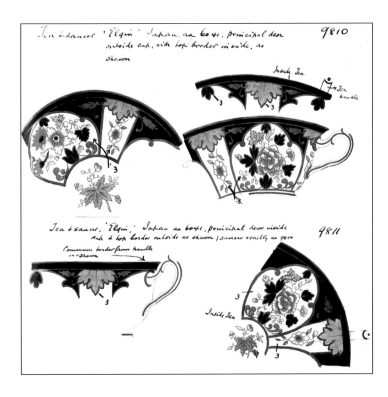

A variation of an 1898 Crown Derby pattern for a cup and saucer made between 1926 and 1930. (*Royal Crown Derby Museum*)

Minton miniature tea service consisting of teapot, sugar bowl, jug and bread-and-butter plate. (*Minton Archives, Royal Doulton plc*)

mother-of-pearl, crystal or silver. By the end of the century matching sets of up to 43 pieces were being manufactured and included 12 teacups, 12 saucers (designed for use with both tea cups and coffee cups), 6 (or sometimes 12) coffee cups, a teapot with cover and stand, a sugar dish with cover and stand, a slop basin with stand, a tea canister with cover, a milk pot with cover and a spoon tray. Plates did not generally form part of the set, although, after 1750, some sets did include two, presumably for thin slices of bread and butter.

For a while in the second half of the eighteenth century, the increasing demand for tea wares led the English East India Company to include a request for '80 teasets' in 1775 with their order for 1,200 teapots, 2,000 covered sugar bowls, 4,000 milk pots and 480,000 cups and saucers. Many of these inevitably found their way into aristocratic homes. However, with the price of tea still high, and perhaps with competition stiffening from European porcelain-makers, the market for Oriental porcelains slowed right down. The company informed its agent in 1690, 'China goods of all sorts are in a very low esteem here . . . That trade hath been much overlaid of late and must be declined for a while to recover its reputation.'

The trade in table wares continued to cause problems, and as late as 1781 the East India Company's records show that, despite the demand for matching sets of tea things, packers in China often shipped an odd mixture:

We think it necessary to repeat, we continue to sustain very heavy losses by the china ware being much false packed, that is to say the goods have come of a variety of patterns, where they should all have been alike particularly in Table and other sets – in some cases there have been so many patterns and so very different from each other that they could not possibly have been put up to sale in sets but have been obliged to be sold as odd pieces. We seldom open a parcel of sets especially Table and tea, but we find several articles different from the Pattern.

Poorer families who could not possibly afford the fine cups, pots, spoons and sugar nippers pooled resources at tea-drinking occasions. In 1756, Jonas

Hanway, in *A Journal of Eight Days' Journey to which is Added an Essay on Tea*, described the situation in poor rural areas 'where the people are so poor, that no one family possesses all the necessary apparatus for tea, they carry them to each others' houses to the distance of a mile or two and club together materials for this fantastic amusement'.

In the novel *Northanger Abbey*, which was begun in 1798, Jane Austen highlighted the concern of the day with owning the right sort of china:

The elegance of the breakfast set forced itself on Catherine's notice when they were seated at table, and luckily it had been the general's choice. He was enchanted by her approbation of his taste, confessed it to be neat and simple, thought it right to encourage the manufacture of his country, and for his part, to his uncritical palate, the tea was as well-flavoured from the clay of Staffordshire, as from that of Dresden or Seve [Sèvres]. But this was quite an old set, purchased two years ago. The manufacture was much improved since that time; he had seen some beautiful

Part of an Art Deco 1930s teaset by Shelley, recognisable by its characteristic solid triangular cup handles. (*Author's Collection*)

specimens when last in town, and had he not been perfectly without vanity of that kind, might have been tempted to order a new set.

However, it was the introduction of 'afternoon tea' in the early years of the nineteenth century that led to the true burgeoning of manufacture of tea sets and all related tea wares. Rich and poor alike wanted, indeed needed, at least one tea set in fine china. Stately homes often had several and brought out a different one to suit the room or the weather or simply the

By the mid-1900s, every middle- and upper-class household owned at least one tea set. This stereograph is by Alfred Silvester and was taken between 1855 and 1860. (*Courtesy of the Trustees of the V&A*)

occasion. Mrs Armstrong, writer of books on etiquette, told readers of *Good Form* in 1889: 'Tea is offered to the visitors on their arrival. A pretty little afternoon tea service is placed upon a small table and there is plenty of rolled bread and butter, as well as biscuits and cakes . . . The hostess can either sit near the table or stand beside it whilst she pours the tea. If a gentleman happens to be present, it is his duty to hand the cups to the ladies; if not this office falls to the lot of the daughters of the house.'

Poorer country folk dreamed of possessing at least one pretty tea set for those special occasions when tea was to be served 'properly'. Flora Thompson captured the sense of eager anticipation among the villagers at the prospect of a visit from the travelling salesman to the village in *Lark Rise to Candleford*:

It was the first visit of a cheap-jack to the hamlet and there was great excitement . . . And what bargains he had! The tea service decorated with fat, full-blown pink roses: twenty pieces and not a flaw in any one of them. The Queen had purchased its fellow for Buckingham Palace, it appeared. The teapots, the trays, the nest of dishes and basins . . . Then the glorious unexpected happened. The man had brought the pink rose tea-service forward again and was handing one of the cups round. 'You just look at the light through it . . . Ain't it lovely china, thin as an eggshell, practically transparent, and every one of them roses hand painted with a brush.'

Afternoon tea in the drawing room at Saltram House, Devon. The table is set with the author's white-and-gold tea set, which belonged to her grandmother. (*National Trust Photographic Library/Andreas von Einsiedel*)

The royal household, on the other hand, has always been fully equipped with whatever china wares were called for and can select a set to suit the decor and the occasion. In May 1930 *Home Notes* told its readers: 'When the Queen gives an afternoon party at Buckingham Palace . . . Tea is laid in the Green drawing room and the wonderful green-and-white Spode service is used.'

Sadly today, many people have hidden their tea wares in the loft or sold them to antique dealers, as they no longer serve tea in the traditional style. But there can be no doubt that for those who have treasured and still use their 'old-fashioned' tea things, tea time is a far more pleasurable occasion. For it involves not just the satisfaction of thirst and a need for recuperation but the visual pleasure of the beautiful tea things and the spiritual refreshment of the ceremony of brewing.

18
tea cosies

'Warming the Pot'

The idea of covering the teapot with a padded or knitted 'cosy' developed during the nineteenth century at a time when more and more people were serving tea at breakfast and during the afternoon. The Victorians were responsible for taking the idea of elegant drawing-room tea and embellishing it with fancy foods, charming table wares, pretty linens and teapot-hugging cosies. The cosy seems to have started life as a hand-knitted tea-time extra, crafted by those who had the time, skill and inclination to stitch and embroider, knit and crochet. Some were simply and practically made from heavy linens and cotton; others were crafted from rich, indulgent velvets, satins, silks and lace and decorated with elaborate embroidery in satin threads or brightly coloured wools, or adorned with tassels and fringes, ruffles and beadwork. Those early cosies did not have carefully positioned openings for spouts and handles and it was not until the introduction of the 'bachelor tea cosy', which incorporated these openings, that tea could be poured without having to lift the warming cover.

'Never trust a man who, when left alone in a room with a tea cosy, doesn't try it on.'
Billy Connelly, Scottish comedian

As the popularity of the cosy grew, many were commercially produced and the choice varied from elegant domes of rich expensive fabrics over padded inners to hinged handbag-like containers that folded up to enclose the teapot in a warm and secure nest. And perhaps more popular than these, crinoline ladies stood imperious with porcelain head and upper body fitted neatly into ruffled knitted skirts through which handle and spout peeked daintily out. The dainty porcelain half-ladies were manufactured by most of the major potteries in Germany, France and England, often in the image of

A tea cosy that was suggested as a very suitable Christmas gift by the magazine *Beauty and Fashion*, on the home pages of the 19 December 1891 edition.

VICTORIAN TEA TIME

It is interesting to speculate whether Anna Maria, the 7th Duchess of Bedford, had any idea how her mid-afternoon cup of tea was going to change British society for ever. For, after all, once she had established the fashion for little tea gatherings at 4 or 5 o'clock, almost every other household in Britain began to copy the idea and hold tea parties of their own. This was the time of the rise of the middle classes, and, in their attempts to appear as wealthy and grand as the members of the upper classes that they emulated, middle-class ladies gave as many elegant afternoon teas as the aristocracy. It was the perfect afternoon entertainment. The men were at work or at their clubs, tea did not demand a huge budget, 2 hours was just long enough to catch up on the latest gossip and fashion, and one did not need a large staff to hand tea to a few lady visitors. It suited everyone.

famous characters such as Emma Hamilton, Marie Antoinette and Sarah Bernhardt. The little 3-in-high bodies had crinoline skirts added in the factory to create ready-made cosies, or they were sold to ladies who had the skill to crochet or knit the cosy-skirt at home. Tiny holes in the porcelain around the waist allowed the necessary stitches to be passed neatly through to keep body and cosy together.

The 19 December 1891 edition of *Beauty and Fashion* suggested the following to readers as a Christmas gift: 'A useful remembrance of the cheery season would be one of the teapots and cosies as used in China. The present consists of a mandarin or blue and white teapot, with a portable case of rattan cane, padded inside with cloth. Tea kept in these cosies does not lose its heat for hours. Three sizes are obtainable, costing 5s 6d, 7s 6d, and 10s 6d each.' The magazine was quite wrong, however, in making a connection between tea cosies and China.

Embroidered satin cosy, 1940s. (*Author's Collection*)

Gradually during the second half of the twentieth century, the home-made look of knitted cosies became outdated and so lost its popularity and today a more ordinary (in fact, rather dull) style seems to be preferred. Sadly, most modern, commercially produced cosies are not nearly as thickly padded as their predecessors and antique cosies (if you can find them) are far more efficient – and certainly more interesting and attractive. Antique linen dealers often stock extremely pretty Victorian cosies of delicate lace fitted neatly over a thick inner pad, and

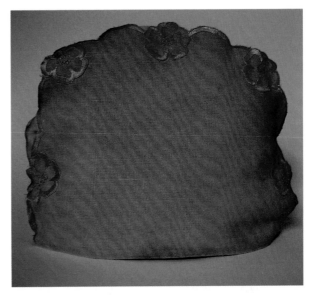

Small, pink linen cosy designed to fit a one-person breakfast teapot, 1940s. It has a matching tray cloth. (*Author's Collection*)

occasionally a hunt around markets and antique malls produces some wonderfully creative and flamboyant cosies that once added a little frivolity to Victorian and Edwardian tea tables.

A cosy from a 1910 Liberty's catalogue, made to fit over almost any shape teapot. (*Museum of Domestic Architecture*)

'Pretty Specimens of Fancy Work'

From an inventory for Knole House in Kent in 1773, it seems that napkins for use during tea-drinking occasions were already an important part of a grand household's store of linen:

> Linnen necessary for Knole 1773
> 4 dozen Bird Eyed Tea Napkens [napkins made in two-colour, double-knit fabric].

In the seventeenth and eighteenth centuries, tables were not covered with a cloth, but, as the popularity of elegant little tea meals grew through the nineteenth century, dainty linen and lace cloths were unfolded and fluttered over wooden tables before cups and saucers, side plates and tea-time cutlery were set in place.

All manner of designs and styles were offered by the linen companies or were worked at home. In October 1891 the 'Shops and Shopping' pages of *Beauty and Fashion* magazine reported: 'Now that the long evenings are

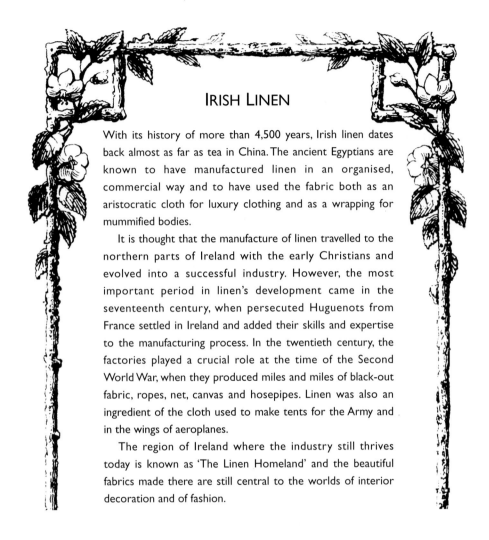

IRISH LINEN

With its history of more than 4,500 years, Irish linen dates back almost as far as tea in China. The ancient Egyptians are known to have manufactured linen in an organised, commercial way and to have used the fabric both as an aristocratic cloth for luxury clothing and as a wrapping for mummified bodies.

It is thought that the manufacture of linen travelled to the northern parts of Ireland with the early Christians and evolved into a successful industry. However, the most important period in linen's development came in the seventeenth century, when persecuted Huguenots from France settled in Ireland and added their skills and expertise to the manufacturing process. In the twentieth century, the factories played a crucial role at the time of the Second World War, when they produced miles and miles of black-out fabric, ropes, net, canvas and hosepipes. Linen was also an ingredient of the cloth used to make tents for the Army and in the wings of aeroplanes.

The region of Ireland where the industry still thrives today is known as 'The Linen Homeland' and the beautiful fabrics made there are still central to the worlds of interior decoration and of fashion.

approaching, we shall be looking out for pretty specimens of fancy work, which always serve to pass the hours pleasantly; while we can at the same time enjoy a cosy chat over the fire without displacing the stitch. New designs in fancy tea cloths for the five o'clock meal have come in full beauty, and surpass any that have been exhibited hither to . . . Afternoon tea cloths of lighter species look very artistic if worked in the Hungarian embroidery style, plenty of which can always be seen at the deposit in Regent Street.'

Tea tray laid with lace-edged white linen tray cloth that beautifully sets off the tea wares and foods. (*National Trust Photographic Library/Andreas von Einsiedel*)

While small round or square cloths decorated little low tables in the drawing rooms or in the garden, a long table for a buffet afternoon was covered with a plainer damask cloth that would set off the gleaming silver urn, the porcelain cups and saucers, the silver bowls of sugar and jugs of milk and all the cake stands and plates that tempted guests with sandwiches, Victoria sponges, shortbread biscuits, little strawberry tartlets, fruit cakes and petits fours. For a 'high tea', as *The New Book of Etiquette* by A Lady in Society, 1907, directed, 'a white cloth is always laid on the table . . . and on it down the centre are placed flowers and in summer, fruits'.

Table linens follow the same changes in taste and style as all other household furnishings and tea-time tablecloths have also been stitched from fabrics of pastel tints, bright colours, soft ivory shades and embellished with printed patterns, embroidered cottage gardens and crinoline ladies, cross-stitch borders, intricate drawn thread-work swirls and scrolls, foliage, flowers and birds. Flora Thompson described the working-class, cottage tea table in *Lark Rise to Candleford*: 'When the men came home from work they would find the table spread with a clean whitey-brown cloth, upon which would be knives and two-pronged steel forks with buckhorn handles.' From a more aristocratic milieu,

The author's Tea-Time tea shop in Clapham, London, which she opened in 1983 with two friends, David Holmes and Clifford Lee. The 1930s hand-embroidered tablecloths created an attractive, nostalgic ambience. (*Author's Collection*)

Lesley Lewis comments in *The Private Life of a Country House, 1912–1939* (1980) that in the Edwardian period 'The fashion in tablecloths changed from plain white to a shade called ecru, both lightly embroidered, then to coarser linen with coloured stripes.' However, nothing is so effective or appealing at tea time as crisp, white linen and lace. As May Sinclair describes in *A Cure of Souls* (1924): 'At that moment, the parlour-maid came in, bringing the tea things. There was a flutter of snow-white linen and the pleasant tinkle of china and of silver, and a smell of hot butter.' In the early part of the twentieth century, tablecloths for tea were known as teacloths, but that name today is more commonly used for the cloths with which we dry dishes.

A design for an afternoon tea-table cloth, illustrated in an edition of *The Needlewoman*, 1930s. (*Museum of Domestic Architecture*)

To dab the crumbs from the lips or spots of jam, butter or cream from the fingers, little tea-time napkins were essential. As American *Vogue's Book of Etiquette* directed in 1935: 'Besides the tea tray, there should be a pile of small plates with a tea napkin (smaller than a luncheon napkin) between each plate.'

A pattern for a crochet-lace edging for a white linen tablecloth, illustrated in *The Needlewoman*, 1930s. (*Museum of Domestic Architecture*)

An elaborate, lace-edged doily, designed to create an attractive border around the food it surrounded, from an edition of *The Needlewoman*, 1930s. (*Museum of Domestic Architecture*)

Such napkins were folded into triangles and set ready on the table, either to the left of the side plate or actually on the plate, often with a small tea knife or pastry fork placed on top of it.

Victorian and Edwardian ladies often arranged bread and butter and cakes not directly on to the china plates, but on to lace doilies that sat on the plate and created a lacy surround for the food. The name comes from the celebrated draper Mr Doily, who had a shop in the Strand in the seventeenth century. His name was originally given to a light linen fabric used to make petticoats and similar garments, and then in the eighteenth century it was applied to table napkins. Presumably the little cloth that now sits under cakes developed from the napkin, and so the name gradually attached itself to the round flat doily. Today's paper doilies are infinitely more convenient but have far less charm than the lace varieties of those days. A 1923 edition of Mrs Beeton's *Household Management* instructed ladies, 'Thin bread and butter, sandwiches, cakes, petits-fours and sometimes fresh fruit are all the eatables given. These are daintily arranged on plates, spread with lace doilies, and placed in a cake-stand or on a convenient table.' The prettiest cloths for tea today are still the white or ivory lace-edged or embroidered linens to be found in antique markets. They have more charm than modern cloths and make a perfect backdrop for all the tea things and the food.

'The Daintiest One Can Afford'

In 1923, in the USA, Della Thompson Lutes wrote in her book on etiquette, *The Gracious Hostess*, 'The appointments for the tea table should be the daintiest one can afford.' She then described all the equipment necessary to create an elegant tea table – most of which have been discussed in earlier chapters of this book. However, over the years, various tea-time extras have been designed and introduced to meet different needs, both in and out of the home.

Cake Baskets

Although afternoon tea did not become a recognised event until the 1830s or 1840s, and thin slices of bread and butter were the normal offering with tea, hostesses had occasionally served a variety of sweetmeats with tea during the previous century. Oval cake baskets (also used as bread baskets) in pierced silver, or fashioned from silver wire, date from the mid-eighteenth century and were designed, with their rolled-back rims, to show off the contents both

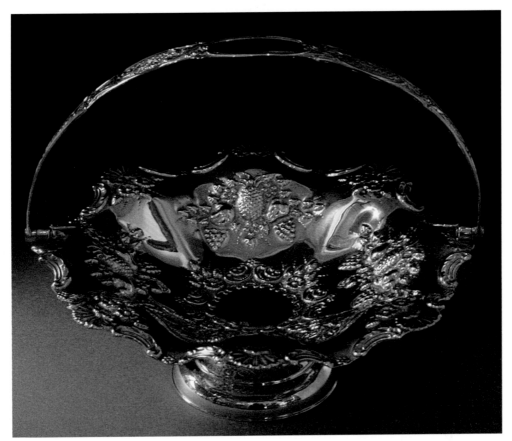

A Victorian silver cake basket designed to show off the contents to their best advantage. (*Honey Tilly*)

from above and through the open silverwork of the sides of the basket. The earliest were decorated with fruits and foliage, scrolls, cherub heads and eagles. Later examples featured sheaves of wheat, flowers and vine leaves and, in the 1780s and 1790s, two-handled baskets were fashionable. These charming openwork containers with their delicate lattice effect remained popular until about 1825 and then, as afternoon tea services became more widely available, flat plates for bread and butter and for cakes were purchased as an integral part of the tea set.

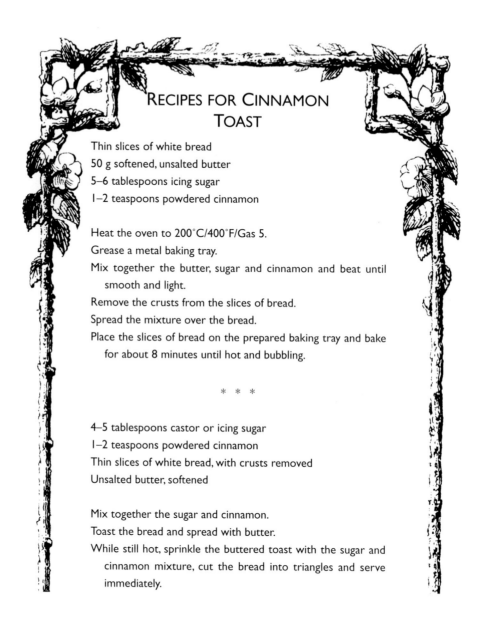

RECIPES FOR CINNAMON TOAST

Thin slices of white bread
50 g softened, unsalted butter
5–6 tablespoons icing sugar
1–2 teaspoons powdered cinnamon

Heat the oven to 200°C/400°F/Gas 5.
Grease a metal baking tray.
Mix together the butter, sugar and cinnamon and beat until
    smooth and light.
Remove the crusts from the slices of bread.
Spread the mixture over the bread.
Place the slices of bread on the prepared baking tray and bake
    for about 8 minutes until hot and bubbling.

* * *

4–5 tablespoons castor or icing sugar
1–2 teaspoons powdered cinnamon
Thin slices of white bread, with crusts removed
Unsalted butter, softened

Mix together the sugar and cinnamon.
Toast the bread and spread with butter.
While still hot, sprinkle the buttered toast with the sugar and
    cinnamon mixture, cut the bread into triangles and serve
    immediately.

Cake Stands

Since afternoon tea was served in drawing rooms with guests seated
comfortably in armchairs, sofas and chaises longues, rather than around a
dining table in dining rooms and kitchens, there was a lack of table space for
all the plates that brought sandwiches, scones, muffins, hot cinnamon toast,

biscuits, pastries and cakes to accompany the cups of tea. And so the cake stand evolved.

Some were light pieces of furniture made in wood or rattan, designed to stand on the floor and could be easily moved into place at tea time. These had three hinged shelves each large enough to hold a cake plate and, when not in use, folded vertically upwards. The stand then sat neatly against the wall or was tucked away in a tidy corner ready to be brought out at the next tea party.

Other cake stands, often fashioned in silver, were designed to stand on the table and display the tea-time treats on two or three layers. This type of stand is still very popular in hotel tea lounges and tea rooms, as it allows the presentation of several different types of food in generous quantities without taking up all the table space needed for cups, saucers, plates and teapots.

Muffin Dishes

As the variety of food offered at tea time developed during the nineteenth century, new items of table ware were created to allow the easier service of such delicious warm treats as hot buttered toast, muffins and crumpets, warm scones and spicy cinnamon toast. Muffin dishes, in porcelain, stoneware or silver, were cleverly designed with a hollow chamber in the base that could be filled with hot water and then sealed with a little cork, a flat section that sat above the heat and a domed lid that kept the heat in and so made sure that hot buttered muffins and crumpets really were very warm when served. By the 1920s and 1930s, afternoon tea sets often included a matching muffin dish.

Muffineers

This delightful item of tea ware developed from the traditional sugar caster and was designed for shaking a liberal covering of cinnamon-flavoured sugar on to hot buttered toast or toasted muffins. Early muffineers were

'In winter an Art Nouveau covered dish with a blister-pearl finial was put near the fire on a brass tripod and this contained hot scones, buns, crumpets, hot-buttered toast or anchovy toast. A wooden cakestand, its three circular tiers folding flat on a rod when put away, held plates of usually rather plain cakes and biscuits.'
Lesley Lewis, *The Private Life of a Country House 1912–1939*, 1980

An elegant three-tier cake stand designed to save space on the tea table but allow the colourful display of sandwiches, scones and pastries. (*Thomas Goode*)

'Tea was brought in for the girls' benefit, and Kitty poured it out, spilling the milk over the cloth, and covering the wet spot with the muffin dish with admirable presence of mind. She felt so much at home that she helped herself to cake a second time without being asked, drank three cups of tea, and only refrained from a fourth because the pot was drained.'

Mrs George de Horne Vaizey,
A Houseful of Girls (1902)

A silver muffin dish, 1930s. It is layered inside to allow boiling water to fill the base and keep buttered muffins and crumpets warm. (J. & S. Stodel)

Muffineer designed by French silversmith Jean Puiforcat in about 1935 and made in 1949 by Elkington & Company of Birmingham. (J. & S. Stodel)

usually vase-shaped, stood about 4 in high and had low-domed covers that were punched with fine circular holes and decorated with embossing or engraving. Later they became much plainer and then disappeared altogether from the tea table.

Pastry Forks

These neat little three-pronged forks developed from Victorian dessert knives in the second decade of the twentieth century. To allow the user gently to break into a slice of Madeira cake, fruit tartlet or chocolate gateau, the first two prongs were sensibly fused together to give a stronger, wider cutting edge. Traditionally they are used only at tea time and only for cakes and pastries, never for sandwiches or scones. The forks generally came in boxed sets of six, sometimes

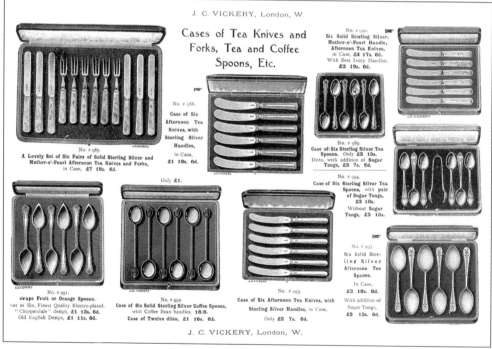

A selection of tea knives and forks, tea and coffee spoons, from J.C. Vickery's catalogue, 1922–3. (John Pearman)

158

THE BEST WAY TO SERVE AN ENGLISH MUFFIN

Muffins are made with a slight split right around the middle. The Victorian way to serve muffins is to toast them whole until both sides are golden and crusty. Then insert the thumb and fingers into the split and pull the muffin apart so that the dough in the middle is revealed, soft and steamy. Spread immediately with butter and eat with jam or honey, cheese or gentleman's relish.

with a larger three- or four-pronged cake-serving fork. Like all table wares, designs followed fashion, and antique markets and silver dealers often have examples of Art Nouveau, Edwardian and Art Deco forks to offer collectors.

Tea Knives

Like pastry forks, tea knives started to appear after 1910 and also came in boxed sets of six. Just long enough to sit tidily on a tea plate, their short blades were perfect for spreading butter on toasted muffins or jam and clotted cream on warm scones. Tea time is a meal that is eaten with the fingers rather than the knives and forks used at other meals. Sandwiches, scones and biscuits are lifted to the mouth with the fingers, cakes and scones are cut or spread with the tea knife but never with the knife and fork together. To eat sticky, indulgent pastries, the pastry fork is held in the right hand with the curve of the prongs facing upwards and then used to break off bite-sized pieces of cake and transfer them to the mouth.

The handles of tea knives can add a splash of colour to the tea table. Although early examples were usually silver or mother-of-pearl, with the development of Bakelite and other plastics, tea knives began to appear with brightly coloured handles that could be matched to china and linen accessories.

THE LONDON COLISEUM.

ONE OF THE
TEA ROOMS.

To add to the enjoyment, the possession of Oriental porcelains gave tea-drinkers in Europe and North America a sense of mystical connection to the origins of the fashionable herb. As Francis Saltus Saltus wrote in his tribute poem 'Tea' in the nineteenth century:

'Thy amber-tinted drops bring back to me
Fantastic shapes of great Mongolian towers,
Emblazoned banners, and the booming gong;
I hear the sound of feast and revelry,
And smell, far sweeter than the sweetest flowers,
The kiosks of Pekin, fragrant of Oolong!'

A 1905 postcard of Fuller's Coliseum Tea Rooms in London. (*Author's Collection*)

Classic Royal Crown Derby teapot known as 'Old Imari', based on a pattern from 1882 and still made today. (*Royal Crown Derby Museum*)

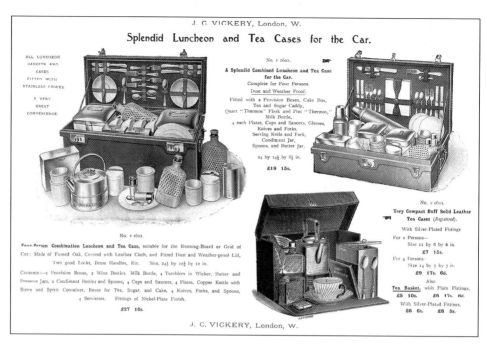

A selection of tea baskets available from J.C. Vickery's catalogue 1922–3. (*John Pearman*)

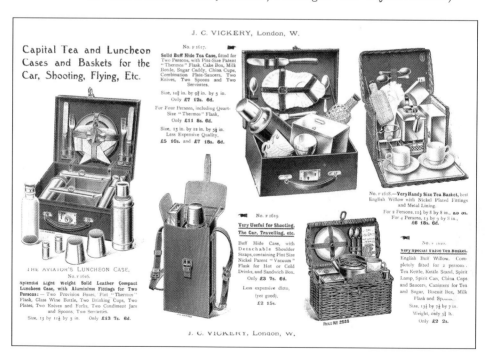

Afternoon tea set out in The Promenade at The Dorchester Hotel, London. (*The Tea Council*)

Tea Hampers

By the twentieth century, taking tea in the afternoon was an everyday occurrence for many people, whether or not they were at home at the right time. And so tea baskets were offered on trains, tea was served on sight-seeing flights over London and picnic hampers were loaded into the backs of cars and at 4 o'clock unloaded and laid out for afternoon tea in the corner of a field or by a river. No matter the location. When the clock stood at 4, everything stopped for tea!

A clever arrangement of shelf and tea basket that allowed passengers on trains to enjoy afternoon tea during their journey in the late 1890s. (From *Beauty and Fashion*, 27 June 1891)

Hornimans
Speciality Teas.
A taste to suit your style.

Darjeeling
A delicate tea
enhanced by its elusive
muscatel flavour.

Other fine teas in the Hornimans range:

Assam Richness and depth of flavour to stimulate the palate.

Earl Grey A fine tea, subtly scented with essence of Bergamot.

Lapsang Souchong China teas with a light, smoky flavour.

Ceylon A fragrantly distinctive tea, with a fine bouquet

Appendix

Places around the World of Interest to Tea-lovers

Britain

BETTY'S CAFÉ TEA ROOMS
1 Parliament Street
Harrogate
North Yorkshire HG1 2QU
Tel: 01423 502746

Betty's also has establishments in York, Ilkley and Northallerton. The tea rooms all have a wonderful traditional feel and the shops at each location sell a fantastic range of cakes, chocolates, teas and coffees.

BIRD ON THE ROCK TEA ROOM
Abcott
Clungunford
Shropshire SY7 0PX
Tel: 01588 660631

Doug and Annabel Hawkes own and run this most attractive of British tea rooms. With its genuine 1930s decor, a selection of teas that is carefully chosen and beautifully served and its own little tea plantation, this is a must for all tea-lovers.

THOMAS GOODE
19 South Audley Street
London W1Y 6BN
Tel: 020 7499 2823

Wonderful selection of porcelains and other table wares.

H.R. HIGGINS LTD
79 Duke Street
London W1M 6AS
Tel: 020 7629 3913

Retail tea shop in St James's, one of London's smartest shopping areas, selling a very good range of world teas.

NORWICH TEA AND COFFEE SHOP
33 Orford Place
Norwich NR1 3QA
Tel: 01603 760790

On the ground floor, the retail shop sells an excellent range of loose teas from around the world, and the first-floor tea room serves lunches and teas from Monday to Saturday.

NORWICH CASTLE MUSEUM
Norwich NR1 3JU

The museum has a specially created gallery that displays more than 3,000 British tea pots and the silver department also owns some wonderful pieces – kettles, pots, dishes etc.

JOHN PEARMAN
The Mall
Camden Passage
Islington
London N1 0PD
Tel: 020 7359 0591

Beautiful porcelains from Britain, Europe and China and a selection of glassware. John's shop is situated in The Mall at Camden Passage, a converted coach house with specialist porcelain shops. Camden Passage itself is a collection of little streets full of stalls and shops selling silverwares, porcelain, strainers, tea knives, caddy spoons etc., as well as other antiques.

ROYAL DOULTON VISITOR CENTRE
Nile Street
Burslem
Stoke-on-Trent
Staffordshire ST6 2AJ
Tel: 01782 292434

Visitors can make a tour of the factory, learn more about Royal Doulton and Minton in the Sir Henry Doulton Gallery and take tea in the restaurant.

S. & J. STODEL
Vault 24
London Silver Vaults
Chancery Lane
London WC2A 1QS
Tel: 020 7405 7009
Website: www.chinesesilver.com

Stephen and Jeremy Stodel offer the largest selection of Chinese silver, particularly tea wares, in Europe, and also stock caddies, teapots, silver tea kettles, muffin dishes etc. from Britain and other parts of Europe.

THE TEA HOUSE
15 Neal Street
London WC2H 9PU
Tel: 020 7240 7539

One of London's best retailers in the fashionable area of Covent Garden. The shop is small but manages to cram a lot in — teas, including expensive Jasmine Pearls and other Oriental gems, herbals, brewing equipment, teapots, books, foods etc.

HONEY TILLY
4/5 Pierrepoint Arcade
Pierrepoint Row
Camden Passage
Islington
London N1 8EF
Tel: 020 7359 4127

A comprehensive selection of British silver including teapots, urns and kettles, cake stands, muffin dishes, milk jugs, butter dishes etc.

R. TWINING & CO.
216 Strand
London WC2R 1AP
Tel: 020 7353 3511

Still in the same location as the first shop that opened in 1706, the shop sells loose teas and coffees, books, teapots, tea-related gifts etc. and at the back there is a small museum of Twining's archive material.

THE VICTORIA AND ALBERT MUSEUM
Cromwell Road
London SW7 2RL
Tel: 020 7942 2000

Wonderful collections of silver and porcelain as well as displays of the decorative arts through several centuries in Britain.

THE WILLOW TEA ROOMS
17 Sauchiehall Street
Glasgow G2 3EX
Tel: 0141 332 0521

and

97 Buchanan Street
Glasgow G1 3HF
Tel: 0141 204 5242

Both shops take visitors back to the days of Kate Cranston when she opened the first of her tea rooms in the 1870s. Tea is served in rooms decorated in the style of Charles Rennie Mackintosh.

ST JAMES'S TEAS
202 Blackfriars Road
London SE1 8NJ
Tel: 020 7401 0630

The company supplies a wide range of speciality teas from around the world to the catering and retail trades in Britain, Japan, North America, Italy and elsewhere. The shop stocks a full range of world teas, books and tea-related items.

WILSON SMITHETT
202 Blackfriars Road
London SE1 8NJ
Tel: 020 7401 0620

Tea brokers for 120 years and suppliers of bulk teas to the trade. Tea-tasting sessions are held every week to give visitors the chance to learn how they work and to take part themselves in sampling teas from around the world.

WHITTARD

73 Northcote Road
London SW11 6PJ
Tel: 020 7924 1888

Whittard also has outlets in most main shopping streets and malls. All the branches sell a good range of loose and bagged teas, as well as teapots, infusers, teapot stands, cosies etc.

Other Parts of Europe

DEMMERS TEEHAUS

Mölker Bastei 5
Vienna 1010
Tel: 0043 533 5995

and

HIGH TEA

Paniglgasse 17
Vienna 1040
Tel: 0043 504 1508

Both these shops belong to Andrew Demmer, whose tea shops and tea rooms offer a large selection of quality teas, teapots, British tea-time foods such as jams,

biscuits etc. and other tea-related gifts. High Tea has a very comfortable and welcoming lounge area where you can relax in a 1940s or 1950s sofa or armchair and admire the extensive collection of old tea caddies.

MARIAGE FRÈRES

13 rue des Grands-Augustins
Paris 75006
France
Tel: 0033 1 40 51 82 50

and

91 rue Alexandre Dumas
Paris 75020
France
Tel: 0033 1 40 09 81 18

The tea rooms are elegantly colonial in style and the menu offers hundreds of different teas and beautiful pastries, tarts and flans. The shop in rue des Grands-Augustins also has a little museum upstairs with a collection of teapots, old packaging items and other interesting tea wares.

LA MAISON DES THÉIÈRES

17 rue de l'Odéon
Paris 75006
France
Tel: 0033 1 46 33 98 96

Sells an excellent selection of Chinese Yixing and Japanese teapots, bowls, cups, teas etc.

FAUCHON – COMPTOIR DES THÉS

30 place de la Madeleine
Paris 75008
France
Tel: 0033 1 47 42 93 74

Holds tea tastings and offers a good choice of Darjeeling and Assam teas, porcelain and earthenware teapots, silver teapots, books etc.

MUSÉE DE DINAN DE LA THÉIÈRE

19 rue de l'Apport
Dinan 22100
France
Tel: 0033 2 96 87 57 09

A very pretty provincial museum filled with teapots and where tea is served among bric-à-brac collected by a true aficionado. Visitors are also allowed access to the owner's library of books on tea.

MUSÉE THOMAS DOBRÉE

18 rue Voltaire
Nantes 44000
France
Tel: 0033 2 40 71 03 50

Documents the journeys made to China by Thomas Dobrée in the eighteenth century.

MUSÉE DE LA COMPAGNIE DES INDES

Citadelle de Port-Louis
Port-Louis 56290
France
Tel: 0033 2 97 82 19 14

History of the French East India Company, seventeenth-century trade, ships, porcelain trade, copied shape and style etc. in French potteries.

BABINGTONS

Piazza di Spagna 23
Rome 00187
Italy
Tel: 0039 6 67 866 027

Established in 1897, this is a little touch of England in the heart of Italy. Located at the foot of the Spanish Steps, the tea room serves traditional English tea-time foods, an excellent range of loose-leaf teas and also has a small retail area selling teas and tea wares.

L'ART DU THÉ

Pfistergasse 7
CH 6003
Lucerne
Switzerland
Tel: 0041 41 240 32 20

Sells loose teas, porcelain and earthenware teapots, eccentric teapots signed by makers, Limoges porcelain, chocolates etc.

China

CHINA TEA MUSEUM
Shuang Feng Village
Longjin Road
Hangzhou
China
Tel: 0086 571 8796 4112

Hong Kong

FLAGSTAFF HOUSE MUSEUM OF TEA WARE
10 Cotton Tree Drive
Central
Hong Kong
Tel: 00852 2869 0690/2869 6690

Japan

THE TEA MUSEUM
3053–2 Kanaya
Kanaya-cho
Haibara-gun
Shizuoka-ken
Japan
Tel: 0081 547 46 5588

Taiwan

NANG KONG TEA MUSEUM
336 Sec 2 Jiau Zuan Street
Nang Kong
Taipei
Tel: (02) 2782 0812

USA

ELMWOOD INN
2–5 East Fourth Street
Perryville
Kentucky 40468
Tel: 001 606 332 2400

The USA's prime tea location. Bruce and Shelley Richardson own and run this stunning venue, where elegant teas are served in their lovingly restored home, which dates back to the American Civil War. Booking is essential. The retail shops sell brilliant loose-leaf teas and all sorts of other goodies – books, food, table wares etc.

HARNEY & SONS LTD
Village Green
PO Box 638
Salisbury
Connecticut 06068
Tel: 001 203 435 9218

One of the oldest established tea companies in the USA. The founder of the company, John Harney, has been a pioneer in teaching others about tea and in supplying the catering trade and retailers with a wonderful range of teas. The company's very attractive shop sells loose-leaf teas and a beautifully selected range of teapots, books and other tea-time extras and table wares.

IMPERIAL TEA COURT
1411 Powell Street
San Francisco
California 94133
Tel: 001 415 788 6080

Tea shop specialising in Chinese teas. Owner Roy Fong edits a useful and interesting newsletter, which is available via the internet, and also organises trips for tea-lovers to China and Taiwan.

Early twentieth-century advertisement for Tower Tea with oversize pottery teapot. (*Author's Collection*)

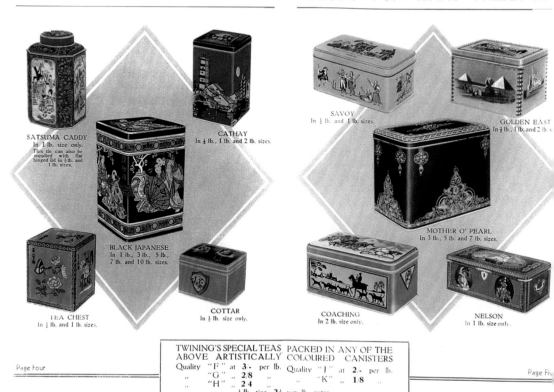

SATSUMA CADDY
In 1 lb. size only.
This tin can also be
supplied with flat
hinged lid in ½ lb. and
1 lb. sizes.

CATHAY
In ½ lb., 1 lb. and 2 lb. sizes.

SAVOY
In ½ lb. and 1 lb. sizes.

GOLDEN EAST
In ½ lb., 1 lb. and 2 lb. s

BLACK JAPANESE
In 1 lb., 3 lb., 5 lb.,
7 lb. and 10 lb. sizes.

MOTHER O' PEARL
In 3 lb., 5 lb. and 7 lb. sizes.

TEA CHEST
In ½ lb. and 1 lb. sizes.

COTTAR
In ½ lb. size only.

COACHING
In 2 lb. size only.

NELSON
In 1 lb. size only.

TWINING'S SPECIAL TEAS	PACKED IN ANY OF THE
ABOVE ARTISTICALLY	COLOURED CANISTERS
Quality "F" at 3.- per lb.	Quality "J" at 2.- per lb.
" "G" " 2/8 "	" "K" " 1/8 "
" "H" " 2/4 "	
½ lb. tins. 2d. per lb. extra.	

Decorative metal caddies designed as Christmas gifts for R. Twining's, 1930s. (*Twinings*)

These Mansheng teapots were highly sought after by collectors of Yixing wares.

172

Bibliography

Armstrong, L. Heaton. *Etiquette and Entertaining*, London, John Long, 1889

——. *Good Form A Book of Everyday Etiquette*, London, White, 1889

Banister, J. *English Silver*, London, Cassell, 1987

Bayard, M. *Hints on Etiquette*, London, Weldon & Co., 1884

Beeton, I.M. *The Book of Household Management*, London, Ward Lock, Bowden & Co., 1892

——. *The Book of Household Management*, London, Ward Lock, Bowden & Co., 1906

Burney, F. *The Journals and Letters of Fanny Burney*, ed. Joyce Hemlow et al., 10 vols, Oxford, OUP, 1972–

Butler, Robin. *The Arthur Negus Guide to English Furniture*, London, Hamlyn, 1978

Chippendale, Thomas. *The Gentleman and Cabinet-Maker's Director*, London, Chippendale, 1754

Chow, K. and Kramer, I. *All the Tea in China*, San Francisco, California, Chiban Books and Periodicals, 1996

Clark, S. and F. *Old Silver Tea Accessories*, Williamstown, 1962

Cosnett, T. *The Footman's Directory, and Butler's Remembrancer*, London, T. Cosnett, 1823

Crunden, J. *The Joyner and Cabinet-maker's Darling, or Pocket Director*, London, Webley, 1770

De Castres, E. *A Collector's Guide to Tea Silver 1670–1900*, London, Muller, 1977

Dower, Pauline. *Living at Wallington*, Ashington, Northumberland Arts Group, 1984

Ehrmann, J.K. *The Book of Tea Caddies*, Vienna, Buchkultur, 1993

Elliston, D. *British Tastes: An Enquiry into the Likes and Dislikes of the Regional Consumer*, London, Hutchinson, 1968

Emerson, Robin. *British Teapots and Tea Drinking*, London, HMSO, 1992

Evans, John C. *Tea in China*, Westport, Connecticut, Greenwood, 1992

Glanville, Philippa. *Silver in England*, London and New York, Holmes & Meier, 1987

Godden, Geoffrey Arthur. *Oriental Export Market Porcelain*, London, Granada, 1979
Goss, S. *British Tea and Coffee Cups, 1745–1940*, Princes Risborough, Shire, 2000
Greenberg, M. *British Trade and the Opening of China 1800–1842*, Cambridge, CUP, 1951
Griffin, Leonard. *Taking Tea with Clarice Cliff*, London, Pavilion, 1996
Heal, Sir A. *The London Furniture Makers from the Restoration to the Victorian Era*, London, Batsford, 1953
Honey, W.B. *European Ceramic Art*, London, Faber & Faber, 1963
Jackson, Sir Charles. *English Goldsmiths and their Marks*, London, Macmillan, 1905
Kakuzo, O. *The Book of Tea*, Rutland & Tokyo, Charles Tuttle, 1956
Kwan, L. *Not All Teas are Created Equal*, Hong Kong, Lee Kwan Tea Trade Ltd, 2001
Ledger, A.P. *Derby Cabinet Pieces and Cyphered Tea Wares*, Derby, Porcelain International Society, 1998
Lewis, Lesley. *The Private Life of a Country House*, Newton Abbot, David & Charles, 1980
Maitland, D. *5000 Years of Tea*, Honk Kong, Pal-Passmore, 1982
Miller, P. and Berthoud, M. *An Anthology of British Teapots*, Bridgnorth, Micawber, 1985
Norie, J. *Caddy Spoons, An Illustrated Guide*, London, Murray, 1988
Oman, C.C. *English Domestic Silver*, London, Black, 1934
Onesimus (Thomas Cosnett). *The Footman's Directory, and Butler's Remembrancer*, London, 1823
Palmer, A. *Moveable Feasts*, London, OUP, 1952
Pettigrew, J. *The Tea Companion*, London, Quintet, 1997
——. *A Social History of Tea*, London, The National Trust, 2001
Reade, Arthur. *Tea and Tea Drinking*, London, Sampson Low & Co., 1884
Scott Thomson, Gladys. *Life in a Noble Household, 1668–1771*, London, Jonathan Cape, 1937
Sinclair, M. *A Cure of Souls*, London, Hutchinson, 1924
Thompson, F. *Lark Rise to Candleford*, Oxford, OUP, 1945
Tschumi, G. *Royal Chef*, London, William Kimber, 1954
Vogue's Book of Etiquette, New York, Doubleday, 1935
Ukers, W.H. *All About Tea*, 2 vols, New York, Tea & Coffee Trade Journal, 1935
Walking, G. *Tea Caddies – An Illustrated History*, London, Victoria & Albert Museum, 1985

Index